DIANA ROSS

GEOFF BROWN

ST. MARTIN'S PRESS
NEW YORK

ISBN 0-312-19932-5

First published in Great Britain by Sidgwick and Jackson Limited.

First U.S. Edition

10 9 8 7 6 5 4 3 2 1

CONTENTS

INTRODUCTION

If an individual's rise from rags to riches, from relative poverty to a position of power, is still at the heart of the American Dream, then the career of Diana Ross is as good an example of that perhaps mythical Dream at work as one could wish to see. Although the now world-famous singer and actress did not exactly spring from the gutters of Detroit, her start in life there certainly had none of the trappings of wealth or privilege.

Closely allied to her story is that of Berry Gordy Jr and his Motown Record Corporation, the label for which Diana has recorded for twenty years. Gordy was the prime architect of her career for almost as long, and he engineered the inexorable expansion of his company to become the corporate reflection of the Dream.

Of course, in an era when a peanut farmer and a second-rate movie actor are elected President of the United States, Diana's attainment of international stardom may seem small beer by comparison. But the stories of both the Motown label and its major woman star are the more potent because the starring roles are all played by blacks.

The progress of Diana from Detroit waif to international superstar in many ways directly corresponds to the twenty-year climb of Motown Records from a cluster of independent local labels to become the biggest-selling, most consistently successful independent label in the world. It was Diana's voice which led the Supremes through a staggering number of hits written and produced by Holland-Dozier-Holland between 1964 and 1967 and which established the label both financially and on the pop charts. Her voice was one whose sound and style, carefully developed in the years leading up to Motown's mid-sixties' breakthrough, became emblematic of the label and, in Britain especially, of black American music in general. Yet Diana's was by no means a typical 'black' voice, and the very fact that it was so different from those readily identifiable as black helped the Supremes, and Motown, to reach the mass white pop market and the 'respectable' adult showbusiness world of cabaret and concert hall.

By 1962 the white pop music market was hungry once more for singing of a more assertive and exciting kind. The traditional pop music writers of

Tin Pan Alley had assimilated and to a large degree dissipated the energy and earthiness of fifties' rock 'n' roll and a new, young generation had no music they could genuinely call their own. The Motown Sound, with Diana Ross as its figurehead, was one of the first of several sounds and styles to move into that gap and satisfy that need. The blending of Ross's recognizable, acceptable voice with the gospel-tinged melodies and harmonies of Motown's writers, the gospel-influenced playing and arrangements of the Motown studio musicians, and the gospel-derived sound values of the label's producers formed the basis of the Motown Sound. That style and sound was the essence of the term 'soul music', by which all black artists' work was soon to be known.

'Soul' referred to the high degree of emotional commitment and personal expression a singer brought to a performance. This quality was something which had been instilled into black singers, almost without exception, from the moment they could walk as far as their local church to take their place in the choir or congregation. Soul music was gospel music's melodies, harmonies and expressiveness combined with secular, sexual lyrics. Previously, secular black American music, known for many years as race music, was rough, tough and aggressive and stood little chance of appealing to a mass white market generally unaccustomed to such wild, abandoned sounds. Gospel, however, had a comparatively sweeter sound while retaining the rhythmic excitement of rhythm and blues, as race music came to be called, and this blend of compelling beat, melodic attractiveness and exciting, inspiring singing was one which Motown, Diana Ross and most black artists in the sixties mixed with great skill.

When we talk of Motown Records we inevitably think of Berry Gordy Jr. Seen as founder and father figure or ogre and Svengali, he won the loyalty and respect of his artists and staff but with many of them there came a sour parting of the ways with dark mutterings from the employee and a stern, patriarchal silence from Mr Gordy. One thing is clear. His personal attention to the development of Diana's career from the early sixties in Detroit to the mid-seventies in Los Angeles virtually assured her accla-

mation as one of the most glamorous stars in show-business and a film star of repute following her powerful acting debut as Billie Holiday in *Lady Sings the Blues*. During that time Gordy had built his label from a small family concern situated in an unprepossessing building in Detroit to the multi-million dollar corporation which now resides in Los Angeles, California.

So before looking at the specific career of Diana Ross, it is necessary to examine both the musical environment from which the Gordy strategy grew and the way in which the Motown Corporation was formed.

In the mid-fifties popular music in America had been blown apart by rock 'n' roll. This hybrid of rhythm and blues and country and western had simmered and boiled over with the apparently sudden appearance of Elvis Presley's first big hit in 1956. He immediately caught the imagination of a young market alienated by and bored with the vacuous outpourings of Tin Pan Alley.

Presley, Little Richard, Fats Domino, Jerry Lee Lewis and, in a sweeter vein, Buddy Holly, set a style for the music that was acceptable to a mass white market. As soon as Tin Pan Alley saw that this new music's popularity wasn't the passing fancy they assumed it to be, the writers began to adapt the style. Thus by the end of the fifties rock 'n' roll existed, in a less raw form, next to more traditional Tin Pan Alley styles of popular music and new dance crazes like the twist.

In Britain, rock 'n' roll had similarly been absorbed into an altered popular music scene which had its own fads and fashions, such as booms in traditional New Orleans jazz and skiffle, as well as its own, home-grown rock 'n' roll stars such as Tommy Steele and Cliff Richard. These singers, however, soon moved into mainstream pop for family audiences.

In the rhythm and blues market in America (in other words records bought only by blacks) there had long been a tradition of group singing far stronger than that in the white pop world. Throughout the fifties doo-wop and tougher rhythm and blues groups such as the Clovers, the Dominoes, the Five Keys, the Five Royales, Clyde McPhatter and the Drifters, the Orioles, the Penguins, the Charms and the Platters co-existed in that market-place alongside the blues heavyweights like B.B. King, Little Walter and Jimmy Witherspoon and jump band artists like Louis Jordan and Wynonie Harris.

Towards the end of the decade the smooth doo-wop and harder rhythm and blues bands had been ousted by Fats Domino, Little Richard and Elvis Presley, who was in the vanguard of white acts intermittently appearing on the black rhythm and blues charts.

One of the singers who enjoyed many rhythm and blues hits in the late fifties – six in the period 1958–9 – was Jackie Wilson. His second hit, 'Lonely Tear-drops', went to number one where it stayed for seven weeks. The song was co-written by Berry Gordy Jr. Gordy had also written Wilson's first chart hit, 'To Be Loved', and this success as a writer encouraged him to set himself up as an independent producer.

He hadn't always been so closely involved with music. His store-owner father and mother lived and worked in Detroit, Michigan. The family was large and close-knit, so much so that his brothers Fuller, Robert and George and sisters Gwen and Esther would all later work at Gordy's record company, and in some cases marry artists and producers on the label; the habit persists today – one of Gordy's daughters, Hazel, married Jermaine Jackson, once of the Jackson Five, now a Motown solo artist.

By the time he moved into record production, Gordy had already tried two of the traditional careers open to blacks in Detroit. He'd boxed and he'd laboured on one of the city's car assembly lines, working at Ford on seat upholstery. But his ear for music led him to run his own record shop, and although it went bust he gained first-hand knowledge of the retail side of the business and could see what types of sound moved most quickly off the shelves.

Gordy started writing with various co-writers, but the most immediately successful partnership was the one struck up with Tyrone (also spelled Tyren and Tyron) Carlo. Together they wrote five of Jackie Wilson's hits – 'To Be Loved', 'Lonely Teardrops', 'That's Why' and 'I'll Be Satisfied' in the United States in 1958–9, and 'Reet Petite' in Britain in 1957.

Those early hits are interesting examples of the direction in which Gordy's aim as a writer and, later, producer and label-owner would be. The British hit was a fast, jaunty, novelty rock 'n' roll song about the perfections of Wilson's girl, sung in an untypical, quirkily excitable style. 'Teardrops', 'That's Why' and 'Satisfied' blended Wilson's high, joyful, gospel-based singing into a pop form with rather more ease. But many of the other Gordy/Carlo collaborations were pure Tin Pan Alley big ballad melodies and arrangements, wholly comforting to white ears and perfect for pop radio. With the perhaps obvious proviso that these were the sort of records that Wilson's record company, Brunswick, wanted him to make, their success must nevertheless have

Marvin Gaye (right) and Stevie Wonder (far right) were instrumental in the establishment of the label in the sixties and its subsequent development through the seventies, both commercially and artistically. Heart-throb Gaye became the label's sex symbol, then its sensitive social commentator with the What's Goin' On *album; Wonder was just what his stage name suggested – a prodigy*

impressed on Gordy, if convincing he needed, that the way to commercial success, financial stability and corporate respectability lay through the ability to form a rhythm and blues market base from which to cross over into the bigger and more lucrative white pop market. This was at the very root of Berry Gordy's strategy: success on a large scale in the white market with black music. He saw at an early stage that sweet, gospel-derived melodies and singing would achieve that. He also realized that big ballads and Las Vegas-style performances would win an older audience missed by the hit singles, and success in that market also became an attractive idea at that time.

Wilson wasn't the only artist with whom Gordy was working then. As well as making demonstration recordings of his songs using a local singer called Eddie Holland, Gordy also became an independent producer in 1958 and recorded 'Got a Job' with the Miracles and 'Come to Me' with Marv Johnson. Gordy had met William 'Smokey' Robinson, the lead singer of the Miracles, in New York when Gordy was sizing up the opposition and the Miracles were looking for a recording deal. The Miracles failed to get a contract but returned with Gordy to Detroit, where he recorded 'Got a Job' (an answer to a 1958 hit titled 'Get a Job' by the Silhouettes) and leased his production out to End Records. The single sold comparatively poorly, but the meeting of Gordy and Robinson was important in the embryonic development of Motown. Robinson, who is still with Gordy and the label as an artist, producer and executive after two decades, flowered into one of the most poetic writers in popular American music in the sixties. His songs not only gave the label many commercial successes but also brought it consistent artistic credibility and contributed much revenue to Gordy's lucrative publishing company, Jobete, even at times when it was fashionable for rock writers to decry Motown's style as repetitive and formularized.

Gordy had more immediate success with his other 1958 protégé, Marv Johnson. Johnson was another local Detroit singer and had worked with a group called the Serenaders. But as a solo singer under the aegis of Gordy he began turning in light, bubbly pop songs which were rather more snappily done than

other records from similar black sources at the time. The initial Gordy/Johnson hits are notable not only for the merry tone they strike but for the instrumentation used, particularly the insistent rapped tambourine, which carries more than a vague suggestion of the Motown Sound to come.

The Marv Johnson hits of 1959–60 – 'Come to Me', 'I'm Coming Home', 'You Got What It Takes' (the only American hit to chart in Britain and Gordy's first big hit as a producer), 'I Love the Way You Love', 'Move Two Mountains' and 'Happy Days' – found Gordy working with new co-writers including Smokey Robinson, Janie Bradford, Berry's sister Gwen, and Eddie Holland, most of whom became an essential part of the labels set up by Gordy.

The young producer/writer became dissatisfied with the arrangement of leasing his productions out to minor companies such as End and larger labels such as Chess (who took the Miracles' 'Bad Girl') and United Artists (Marv Johnson) for pressing and distribution. Cash flow problems were caused by slow royalty payments and low profit margins and the service given was not always reliable, especially when one of the distributing label's own acts required extra attention at the same time. So the Gordy family began setting up its own labels.

Gwen Gordy had formed Anna, named after her sister, in 1959. A Chess-distributed label, it is best remembered for Barrett Strong's version of a Berry Gordy/Janie Bradford-penned hit, 'Money', which came within one place of a number one rhythm and blues hit in January 1960. Although there has been some debate, such as that instigated by John Lee Hooker, the blues singer, about the precise origins of the song – and such debates are frequent in early rhythm and blues song publishing – the single's success was the final spur to Gordy.

Borrowing between six and eight hundred dollars from his family, he moved in 1960 into premises on Detroit's West Grand Boulevard, a rather humbler locale than its name suggests, and named the building Hitsville USA. The Miracles with Smokey Robinson were one of his first signings, along with Eddie Holland. His first label was named Tammy, reputedly after the Debbie Reynolds hit of that name, but because of copyright problems it was changed, via Tammie, to Tamla.

13

The Motown tourists taking the London air in March 1965. Front row, from left: Supremes Florence Ballard, Mary Wilson and Diana, the Vandellas with (right) Martha Reeves. Back row from left: Temptations David Ruffin (glasses and hat), Melvin Franklin, Otis Williams, Paul Williams, Miracle Bobby Rogers (at rear in glasses and hat), Temptation Eddie Kendricks, Miracle Pete Moore, who is partly obscuring Miracle Ronnie White. Where's Smokey Robinson? He's somewhere on the end of that black-gloved, white-raincoated right arm behind Otis Williams

When it became known that the man who'd written hits like 'Money', 'You Got What It Takes' and 'Lonely Teardrops' had set up his own business, the burgeoning black talent of Detroit and its suburbs flocked to the label – in fact, to the labels plural, for the Gordy family had stretched its net wide. Apart from Gwen Gordy's Anna label, her husband-to-be, Harvey Fuqua, had formed the Harvey and Tri-Phi labels. From his previous label, Chess, Fuqua introduced into the scene a singer from the Moonglows named Marvin Gaye. Gaye became not only a solo singer on Gordy's growing roster but also another brother-in-law when he married Anna Gordy.

At the tail-end of 1960 the new Tamla label scored a quick first hit with the Miracles' 'Shop Around', a Gordy/Robinson composition. The record eventually reached the number one spot on the rhythm and blues charts and crossed over on to the pop charts, peaking at number two, and gave the label its first gold record. Here was further proof that Gordy's ear and production touch were attuned to the pop music market, which was by now gaining momentum to become one of the great growth industries of the sixties and early seventies.

The success of 'Shop Around' drew even more black artists to this wholly-owned and run black company where they would clearly feel more at ease. They could be certain that the crucial areas such as A & R and production right through to finished product would be overseen by sympathetic and talented fellow blacks. 'Shop Around' had also proved that Tamla could have national success. Although Detroit was rich in musical talent and raw material, the ambition of the local labels had previously been extremely modest, and the major New York and Philadelphia companies made regular excursions to the motor city shopping for fresh signings.

Gordy began to assemble all the local labels started by his family and in-laws under the banner of his main company, Motown Record Corporation (Motown being an abbreviation of motor town). The Motown label itself started releasing singles in 1960 with, at first, little success, as indeed had happened on Tamla. Early Miracles' sides in 1960 such as 'Way Over There' had only been locally successful.

When Harvey Fuqua's Tri-Phi and Harvey labels got into financial difficulties, Gordy bought them up and thus acquired artists like Marvin Gaye, Junior Walker, the (Motown) Spinners and Shorty Long, and producers such as Johnny Bristol and Fuqua himself; Fuqua was to stay with the company until the late sixties and is now best known as producer of Sylvester. Similarly, when Gwen Gordy's Anna label had been wound up, those acts who did not first join Fuqua went directly to Gordy; notable among them was Barrett Strong, who soon became a house producer there. The contacts Gordy made as a writer served him well, too. Jackie Wilson recommended that the new company sign a group called the Contours, who had come to Wilson's attention simply because his cousin sang with them and had asked for his help and advice.

By staffing most administrative and some creative posts at his fledgling corporation with members of his immediate family, and relying on the natural enthusiasm of young people working at a new company in an exciting business like pop music, Gordy was able to generate a real atmosphere of family feeling, unity and common purpose within the label. And the purpose was to make hit records.

In the first three years the Motown labels' sound was in an almost continuous process of change and flux as the producers searched for an optimum style which would give the corporation an image and identifiable sound, yet still be flexible enough to allow full expressive scope to the often highly individualistic singers they were attracting. This made for a series of excitingly fresh and energetic-sounding records. The Contours' 'Do You Love Me' and the Isley Brothers' 'Twist and Shout', both essentially twist cash-in singles, were sung with great fervour, far more than was heard on the dance craze's smooth theme song by Chubby Checker.

More significant, in respect of later developments, were the eight hits enjoyed by the Marvelettes between 1961 and 1963 on Tamla, the first being the number one rhythm and blues hit 'Please Mr Postman', and the nine hits Mary Wells had on Motown between 1960 and 1963. These hits found Motown getting to grips with how best – or how most profitably – to present women on record.

Although it was less true in rhythm and blues, the record business never seemed quite at home with women artists unless they looked dewy-eyed and submissive. The sexually aggressive stance adopted by rock 'n' roll simply was not the thing for women to attempt. More blues-type singers such as Willie Mae Thornton, Etta James and, especially, Ruth Brown were the exception, but their work rarely spread outside the race market. Now, of course, as society has become more permissive the attitudes struck by women singers – defiant and aggressive or overtly sexually alluring – have become less tentative and restricted. But two decades ago, if women soloists were limited by the moral conventions of the day, women singers in groups were even more restrained. They were little more than an attractive tuneful novelty, even in black music where the vocal group as such was a far more popular entity.

Basically, three types of vocal groups existed among black women. There were those derived from doo-wop, who tended to be seen mostly as the sister companion to a male group; there were the gospel trios, quartets and quintets who had left the sanctity of the church to join the secular rat race; and there were the straight-ahead groups whose music was specifically designed for the expanding post-rock 'n' roll pop market. In the forefront of this last section at the beginning of the sixties were the Crystals and the Shirelles. The Shirelles took a softer, more pliant view of their boyfriends ('Tonight's the Night', 'Will You Love Me Tomorrow', 'Dedicated to the One I Love', 'Soldier Boy' and so on), while the Crystals tended to rejoice in him and celebrate him to the rest of the world ('He's a Rebel', 'Then He Kissed Me', 'Da Doo Ron Ron', 'He's Sure the Boy I Love'). The Shirelles and the Crystals had developed a clear, instantly recognizable style with their writers and producers, and it's arguable that the succession of hits scored by both groups, and later those of the Ronettes produced by Phil Spector, had some contributory effect on the deliberations of Berry Gordy as he sought a strong direction for his labels.

After the successive hit sequences set up by the Marvelettes and Mary Wells, Gordy next found profit in the singing of a Motown secretary who deputized for an ailing singer and was promptly

Gruelling tours made it hard for a girl to look her best at all times despite what the Motown department of charm and deportment might say. Near right: Mary signs the autograph, Diana looks distinctly exhausted. But Marvin Gaye (below right) is cool and hip on British TV show Ready Steady Go *in December 1964, while Little Stevie Wonder (far right) blazes 'Fingertips' on a Motown TV special*

signed as an artist. She was Martha Reeves and her two harmony singers, the Vandellas, produced some fiery performances more in the Marvelettes' bluesy mould than in Wells' lighter style. They sang back-up on Marvin Gaye's early recordings, were put on the Gordy label under their own name, and soon found hit form in 1963 with 'Come and Get These Memories', 'Heatwave' and 'Quicksand'.

So by the end of that year the Motown Corporation had become the third most successful singles label in America, which in music industry terms means the world. And it was by a long, long way the biggest independent record label. Jobete, the music publishing company Gordy had formed early in his writing career, was now an enormous money-spinner and the record company's singles sales accounted for something like seventy-five per cent of record sales revenue. Their album sales were inconsequential by comparison. This was not a worry, however, for singles were still the main medium of all pop record sales, and it was only much later in the sixties that albums would assume greater importance.

Another girl trio had been hanging around the Motown studios and recording with a singular lack of success. They were called the Supremes. The trio had had one small national rhythm and blues hit in December 1962 with 'Let Me Go the Right Way', and one or two of their other early singles did well on a local basis. But their performances were hardly the stuff of which glamorous showbusiness legends could be made.

However, Gordy's producers had been assiduously working towards a distinctive style, and in the late 1963 Motown hits it can be heard coming together. On Martha and the Vandellas' 'Heatwave', written and produced by Brian and Eddie Holland and Lamont Dozier, the song's bouncy inner rhythm, which seems ready to run away with the track, is broken by sudden, emphatic bursts of drumming before careering onward, driven by encouraging, on-the-beat handclaps and tambourine slaps. It sounds like a more urgent expression of the instrumental mixes Gordy used on his Marv Johnson sides.

At about the same time as he put the Vandellas to work with Holland-Dozier-Holland, Gordy decided to team the Supremes with the same producers

because the girls had been complaining about the lack of success and attention they were getting. This partnership took longer to gel. The specific records will be dealt with in Chapter 2 but the basic problem was that the producers couldn't settle on what sound the Supremes' voices made best, and consequently couldn't decide on the type of song and sound that was best suited to them. At one time they would emerge on record sounding like the Vandellas, at another like a less desperate version of the Marvelettes. Before working with Holland-Dozier-Holland, the group had been written for, and produced by, Berry Gordy, Frankie Gorman and Smokey Robinson, whose early track record with the label had been excellent. But even they couldn't find the particular sound and style in which to present the trio's voices.

Yet because the Supremes had never emphatically stamped their vocal personality on those earliest recordings, surely they would be the ideal raw material to mould, from the beginning, into singers whose attractiveness and very facility would be the perfect foil for the gospel-derived melodies and accompaniments that the label and producers had been honing. The Supremes could become the catalyst needed to evolve that house sound and style.

2. IT TAKES...THREE?

Detroit, Michigan. Looking south down the Motor City's North Michigan Avenue. The bright lights were an alluring contrast to the stark industrial side of town, which originally drew blacks away from the southern states

Detroit is a large industrial city on the eastern border of the state of Michigan, situated on the waterway between Lake Erie and Lake Huron. Ontario, Canada is just across the waterway. Detroit's fortune is based on the manufacture of automobiles, mostly Fords. From the car industry's early days when production began expanding at a prodigious rate following the introduction of the family car and the increase in the wealth of the United States, the city acted as a magnet to the unemployed of the agriculturally-based southern states, who were mostly black. The trail from New Orleans and Memphis up to Detroit and Chicago, Philadelphia and Pittsburgh, became a well-trodden one. Detroit soon had a large black population, the fourth largest of any city in the United States.

Inevitably, this huge influx of immigrant workers – predominantly young families, for the elderly generally stayed behind – imposed a tremendous strain on the housing capacity of a city largely unprepared for such a huge invasion. The tenements were crammed to overflowing and the city's housing projects, quickly erected to cope with the swollen population, filled just as quickly.

One of the major housing areas for these immigrants was the Brewster Housing Project, on the north-east side of Detroit, one of the city's less salubrious areas. Diana Ross was one of many of the original Motown artists born and raised in this Project. Her parents, Ernestine and Fred Earle, had six children, three sons and three daughters. Diane, their eldest daughter – it wasn't until she joined Motown that she changed her name to Diana – was born on 26 March 1944. The family was poor but her parents, like most in such a situation, worked, scrimped, saved and did everything in their power to give their children as good a start in life as possible. Although the children often slept three to a bed there always seemed to be another family worse off – like the one next door which had fourteen kids – and as long as Diane had a few cents for a stick of chewing gum or a bar of candy she was happy enough playing around the low-rent Projects with friends, brothers and sisters.

The focal point for virtually all black families was the church. It is rare indeed to discover a black

23

American singer who did not make his or her public singing debut at an inordinately young age in the church choir. Diane was no exception. In fact her family had a strong church tradition – her grandfather, who lived in Alabama and reputedly reached the ripe age of 107, was pastor of the Alabama Bessemer Baptist Church. Diane sang in the church choir in Detroit and at social gatherings there. When she was eight there was one particular party at which she sang and, as often happens, the hat was passed round. When the proceeds were counted she found she'd earned enough to buy a pair of shoes – perhaps an early lesson in the potential earning power of a song.

Aside from church choir singing, the natural tendency was for kids to form vocal groups, imitating their elders and idols whom they heard on the radio, singing on street corners or down subways where the echo enhanced their vocals. Young girls, however, were not widely encouraged to loiter on street corners, unless of course they had already decided upon that profession as the most expedient escape from the ghetto life awaiting them. (Diana in fact used her memories of the local prostitutes, pimps and brothels when creating her Billie Holiday role, and suggested that if she'd fallen for a pimp she too might conceivably have ended up a hooker.)

Among their friends and neighbours were two girls named Florence Ballard and Mary Wilson. Florence had been born in Detroit on 30 June 1944; Mary had been born in Mississippi on 6 March of the same year but moved north to Detroit with her family shortly afterwards. The two, who sang together in their local church choir, decided it would be fun to form a group and thought a trio or quartet would sound better than their duo. Another local friend and hopeful, Eddie Kendricks, recommended Diane to them and the three got together, rehearsed and found their voices blended well enough. This acceptance was some consolation to Diane, for at the age of fourteen she'd been heartily disappointed to fail an audition for a part in her school's musical production. Florence, Mary and Diane added a fourth member, Betty Anderson, and got down to some serious woodshedding. Meanwhile, the girls were progressing through school; Diane developed

an aptitude and passion for dressmaking and designing and set her mind on dress designing as a career. Singing was just something you did in church and at friends' homes.

Kendricks, who'd brought the girls together, was then singing in a group known as the Primes and it was customary in those days for male groups to have female counterparts. So the four girls called themselves the Primettes, and started singing at local clubs and talent shows with the Primes. The Primettes took their act to many of the local Detroit labels. Betty Anderson became disillusioned, left the group and was replaced by Barbara Martin. The new quartet finally landed a contract with the Lu-Pine label.

With writers/producers Richard Morris and Wilmar Davis they recorded several tracks and two singles were released. On 'Tears of Sorrow' Diane sang lead, while on 'Pretty Baby' Mary was the featured vocalist. Although the discs encouraged offers of live work, the Lu-Pine label had a negligible promotional set-up and the records sold poorly. They were far from memorable songs and performances anyway. The group also sang background vocals for other Lu-Pine artists and some of this work eventually surfaced in Britain in 1968 on an Ember album titled *Looking Back*, a very raw, uneven curio.

The girls' brother-group, the Primes, had meanwhile split up. Two of their number, Eddie Kendricks and Paul Williams, had been added to three singers from a group who had the same manager as the Primes, the Distants. This quintet attracted the attention of Detroit's hottest young writer/producer, Berry Gordy, his interest initially being caught by a couple of local hits which the Distants had recorded for the Northern label. Gordy signed the new quintet in 1960 and renamed them the Temptations.

Kendricks suggested that Gordy should hear the Primettes, a recommendation endorsed by Smokey Robinson who had also heard the girls sing. At the time the girls were finishing high school and, despite being reasonably impressed with their performances of a Drifters and a Ray Charles song, Gordy encouraged them to complete their education and perhaps return later. This rebuff aside, it was becoming clear that Diane's wish to become a dress designer, Florence's career as a nurse and Mary's as a teacher might well

Florence, Mary and Diana (far left) grew up in Detroit's Brewster Housing Project, where they met and began singing together in the late fifties. Florence Ballard (left) was born in the Motor City on 30 June 1944. She and Mary were the first to sing together

take second place to singing. But the girls duly finished school and for a while took jobs. Diane worked in Hudson's, a large department store in Detroit, where she was for a time the only black girl employed.

The Primettes continued to hang around the offices of Motown Records. They knew Gordy was interested in them. When they'd auditioned for him he repeatedly asked them to sing the Drifters' 'There Goes My Baby'. But because his early writing and productions had been geared towards male artists such as Marv Johnson, Jackie Wilson, and the Miracles he'd acquired a reputation of being unsure of women singers, and his first women artists, Mary Wells and the Marvelettes, were usually given to other producers and writers to work on. The impression that Gordy believed women artists would create difficulties was thus born.

But the Primettes were persistent. Eventually, a group contracted to add handclaps to a Marvin Gaye session failed to show up and the Primettes stepped into the breach. They were soon doing background vocals and more handclap sessions. Like the use of the tambourine by Motown, handclaps not only gave greater thrust to the rhythm section but provided a direct link to the gospel sound from which the singing and rhythmic impulse of the developing style drew inspiration. Then, in 1961, the Primettes were signed to the label as a group. They continued to do background work, did office chores and became part of the Motown family, socializing after work at Detroit's Twenty Grand club where the company's acts performed and also went to relax.

The Primettes' first single, 'I Want a Guy' backed with 'Never Again', was assigned to the Tamla label and sank like a stone. Although the single appears on the catalogue as having been recorded by the Supremes, it was reputedly the failure of the single which made Tamla decide on changes, albeit of a merely cosmetic nature. The Supremes was just one of a list of names offered to the girls, and Diane became Diana. (Later, when Fred Earle left his wife and children, Diana adopted her mother's maiden name of Ross.)

By now, Gordy's faith in women singers was increasing. The hits of the Shirelles and the Crystals

on other labels, plus those of Mary Wells – five rhythm and blues hits between 1960 and 1962, including two number ones – were proof of the commercial possibilities and, in the case of Wells, a boost to the label's confidence. But that still involved working with one, sweet, distinctive voice out front, though the Marvelettes' stormier records were effectively rousing.

Smokey Robinson's songs and productions with Wells and the Marvelettes had been successful, so he was put to work on the Supremes with Frankie Gorman, who would become one of the Originals group. They were unable to repeat the hit formula, or find a new one. After the Supremes' Tamla single 'Buttered Popcorn'/'Who's Loving You', the group was switched on to the Motown label, where they would remain for the rest of their time together.

The first single on the new label, 'Your Heart Belongs to Me'/'He's Seventeen', fared no better than those before it. Much of the problem was that the company itself was still experimenting with sounds and styles on its new acts. The star names on the roster in those early days – Marvin Gaye, Mary Wells, the Marvelettes, the Miracles – each had an individualistic style not easily moulded. The productions often had the air of a virile compromise between writer, producer and artist.

On the first Supremes singles the lead vocal was swapped around quite regularly and this didn't help to give the group an identity – much of the recorded output of the label's first four years has an unfocussed sound, style and feel in which the best is stunning, the worst unlistenable. 'Your Heart Belongs to Me' was a small local hit in August 1962, but progress was slow and tortuous. Barbara Martin left and the group remained a trio.

In December 1962 the boss, Berry Gordy, started to get things right. His song 'Let Me Go the Right Way' was a small rhythm and blues hit for the Supremes. 'Right Way' had Florence singing lead against a plain, echoey background of guitar, bass, drums and handclaps, with Mary and Diana chirruping their background vocals in a very jerky manner. If one was to play this single to any moderately knowledgeable Diana Ross or Supremes fan, he or she would never guess who was performing on the

record, so untypical is the sound. Its rawness is closer to the Marvelettes or the New York girl groups of the time. But the record had charted, if modestly.

The trio were also working as demo-makers for Martha and the Vandellas and back-up singers for Marvin Gaye. Life wasn't all recording sessions. Gordy had started to send his acts out on the road in various groupings as the Motortown Revue. The five or six acts on each bill would appear in order of chart position at any given week. The Supremes, being the least successful, would usually be first on, which suited the young Diana very well. In later years her eagerness to learn, to know everything about the workings of any project in which she was involved, brought her the nickname, from some, of 'the blotter'. She absorbed everything. This habit would manifest itself in the early sixties on the road. She'd do her act, change, and then sit at the side of the stage studying the other singers and groups, noticing what mannerisms and affectations – physical or vocal – worked best on the audience. By the following night's show she'd have interpolated the best of these tricks into her own performance, and then, of course, going on first became a positive advantage. Anyone who repeated a mannerism would look foolish at best, at worst a cynical plagiarist usurping the simple style of the unknown, bottom-of-the-bill act. As can be imagined, this expression of Diana's desire to learn stagecraft did not exactly endear her to the other acts on the bill. When their patience ran out they had words with Mr Gordy about the alarming competitiveness shown by the opening turn and he put her straight about such matters.

Gordy, however, *was* most anxious for all his artists to learn how to present themselves correctly at all times. As a result he set up an artist grooming department, whose sole task was to teach the young gentlemen and especially the young ladies of the label how to conduct themselves at all times, on and off stage. There was a model agency in Detroit run by a Miss Powell, which went bust. Miss Powell was then hired by Gordy to teach his women artists how to comport themselves – how to walk 'nicely' up and down stairs, how to sit and stand sedately, how to shake hands and make small talk with reporters without giving much away. Others were brought into the department to pass on hints on bowing and curtseying on stage, and how to climb lightly on to a piano for one of those intimate cabaret numbers, as well as putting together the nuts and bolts of a slickly choreographed act with a sufficient amount of arm flailing and the precise number of pirouettes and so forth.

Gordy also insisted on a strict code of personal conduct, especially for his women singers. There must be no hint of scandal of any sort and they were sheltered from drugs, which for so long had plagued the careers of black singers. (It is ironic that the well-tutored Ross should receive acclaim for her portrayal of Billie Holiday, a perfect example of an immensely talented woman ultimately brought down by drug addiction.) And the Motown girls certainly would not be allowed to have boyfriends on the road. They were also given advice on make-up, costume and so on, but as Diana had kept up her passion for fashion these aspects of grooming hardly needed reinforcing. Being the first black girl to work at Hudson's store she had attracted attention and had naturally been particularly fastidious about her appearance. It was the sort of care and pride that remained. Moreover, she took an interest in the clothes the Supremes were to wear on stage, worked with the designers and buyers and had a strong say in how the group would look. All of this grooming was aimed towards one end: to make the Motown acts as acceptable to the cabaret circuit, white market and network television as possible. It certainly paid off.

Back in the studio the writers and producers at Motown still couldn't find the right blend to get the Supremes' career properly rolling. The group's fifth single, 'My Heart Can't Take It No More'/'You Bring Back Memories', failed utterly. Their sixth saw them working on a Smokey Robinson song, 'A Breathtaking Guy'. A slow mid-tempo ballad, it was given fuller production with horns and extra percussion such as bongoes and congas. Diana sang lead, enunciating the lyrics with a clarity so painfully deliberate that she must surely have been rushed from elocution lessons to sing it. But the general cooing delivery and role-playing of the Supremes as supplicant, heart-broken girls indicated how, lyrically, to use their voices. The whole production had the gentle, lilting

mood Smokey had used so well on the string of hits he composed for Mary Wells. Yet that single's flip side illustrated the lack of direction given to the Supremes' recordings at this stage. It was a rare piece of hokum titled 'The Man with the Rock 'n' Roll Banjo Band', about which the least said the better. This indecision and vacillation was, however, soon to change.

One of Berry Gordy's great talents displayed during the first years of Motown was the identifying of skills in others. All the artists he signed in the first years were either completely unknown and new to recording, or else had been spectacularly undistinguished on other labels. This was nowhere better illustrated than by his teaming of the Holland brothers, Brian and Eddie, with Lamont Dozier into a writing and production team. It was to prove a crucial factor in turning Motown from a fast-growing Detroit business into a vast American and international conglomerate by finally giving some sort of homogeneous definition and identity to the label's music.

Eddie Holland had been one of Gordy's earliest signings as a singer. He first worked at the Jobete Music Publishing Company singing on demos, then writing, then recording under his own name. Gordy leased Eddie's records to United Artists. He signed with Gordy's label when it was launched and had one hit in 1962 with 'Jamie', a song which echoed the style of Jackie Wilson, the singer for whom he'd demoed many Gordy compositions. Eddie released another eight singles but only two, 'Just Ain't Enough Love' and 'Candy to Me', had any sort of success. By that time he'd been teamed with his younger brother Brian and Lamont Dozier. Brian had been introduced to Motown by his brother and Gordy had taken him under his wing and helped him develop as a writer and producer. He'd formed a writing/producing partnership with Richard Bateman and had been responsible for hits such as the Marvelettes' 'Please Mr Postman'. When Bateman left Brian began writing and producing with Lamont Dozier. Dozier joined the label after recording as Lamont Anthony for Gwen Gordy's Anna label and Melody. The singles had been bruisingly unsuccessful and Lamont soon concentrated on writing.

Almost immediately this combination began to exhibit the Midas touch. While they didn't exactly turn the singers with whom they worked into graven images, they certainly made their records gold. In 1963 they struck twice in quick succession for Martha and the Vandellas with 'Heatwave' and 'Quicksand', which were essentially variations on the same, or a similar theme. Recycling commercially successful ideas is a pop music convention which the three writers were never above using. In 1964, after agitation from the Supremes for better material, Holland-Dozier-Holland were put to work with the now twenty-year-old singers.

The first fruit was 'When the Lovelight Starts Shining through His Eyes', a rumbustious celebration which shows signs of what was to become the Motown Sound. 'The Sound' was live and vibrant, echoey and exciting. After a strong, horn-led introduction, the drumming settles into its forceful style played with terrific exuberance. Tambourines and handclaps give the track extra drive. The verses are sung over a modified Bo Diddley beat snapping into a normal four-four rhythm in the chorus. Diana's voice settles farther back in the instrumental and backing vocal mix and is far less aggressive than Martha Reeves or the Marvelettes would have been about the song at that tempo. Production and arrangement touches, like the male voices roaring 'rrrruh!' to announce a sudden, quiet, instrumental vamp coloured by lightly played electric organ, set up what was far and away the best Supremes single to that date.

'Lovelight' stayed on the American rhythm and blues charts for eleven weeks, peaking at twenty-three. It sold on to the pop charts and was also the first Supremes record released in Britain. (Between the years 1960 and 1963 Motown singles were released in Britain on the London-American, Fontana and Oriole labels. In 1963 EMI took over the UK distribution and the singles were released on the Stateside label until 1965 when Tamla Motown set up its own label in Britain, distributed by EMI.)

But 'Lovelight' was more than just the first palpable success the Supremes had. With its blend of Diana's higher, flutier vocals and the romping band, the single delivered its punch with a view to that pop

Diana wasn't the immediate regular choice as lead singer. Far left: Florence, flanked by Mary and Diana, sang lead on 'Let Me Go the Right Way', a Berry Gordy song which made the Billboard R & B charts in December 1962. Mary Wilson (left) was the only deep south Supreme, born in Mississippi on 6 March 1944. Her family soon moved north to Detroit

market won by the Crystals through Phil Spector's production in 1962–3 ('Da Doo Ron Ron', 'Then He Kissed Me') and by Martha and the Vandellas and the Marvelettes. The energy that crackled from the model hits was maintained, but the Supremes' vocal tone was softened and made more accessible to white listeners.

The follow-up to 'Lovelight', 'Run, Run, Run', was a track as frantic as its title suggests and simply ran away with all concerned. The accompaniment consisted of mad piano with male background voices in hasty pursuit, which left Diana to tread warily through the desolation. In the light of the hit they'd just scored, and those which were soon to follow, this single is a fascinating exercise in self-destruction, staring, not to say kicking, the gift horse in the mouth. The next single would change all that.

3. I HEAR A SYMPHONY

By the mid-sixties, Motown, under the guiding influence of writers Eddie and Brian Holland and Lamont Dozier (the latter two acting as producers), had developed a distinctive sound and Diana Ross (far left) had emerged as the most adaptable singer for the style. Her slim, gamine look also closely corresponded to that which was becoming fashionable through models such as Twiggy and Jean Shrimpton. She became the 'face' of Motown

Looking back at the years 1964–6 from the perspective of the eighties it is tempting to let the bare statistics of the Supremes' and Motown's achievements in that period speak for themselves. But that would force us to see the company in terms of sales figures and turnover and little else besides. It was now, in fact, that Motown's Sound, and to a large degree soul music itself, was 'invented'.

Of course, the commercial success was phenomenal. It is doubtful whether the circumstances will ever again exist for such a meteoric rise by a single record company. Perhaps the greatest contemporary accolade recognizing the company's arrival was the story in *Newsweek* in 1965, which stated that in the previous year in the United States Motown had released sixty singles of which forty-two had been hits, selling twelve million copies and grossing approximately ten million dollars. To be spoken of in enthusiastic and rather awed terms by a bastion of the white, moneyed middle classes must indeed have been sweet music to Gordy's ears, for these were the people he was seeking to emulate and compete with.

The Supremes were a crucial part of this success. Whenever black music was spoken of in general terms in that period, it was the Supremes who most often sprang to mind, quite simply because they were the most consistent hit-makers and visually the most memorable. Yet although they were so widely associated with these years of rapid commercial expansion, they were not musically the most representative of black artists or of Motown stars. But they had the faces and figures, the carefully manicured personalities and the glamorous image. They were universally acceptable – the months spent in the grooming department at Motown paid huge dividends.

It is fine to be attractive and to make catchy, danceable records, but to rise above that essentially transitory level and become stars who regularly skip across age, class and cultural barriers it is necessary to be rather more, to acquire that intangible, seemingly synthetic quality: glamour. The Supremes did. To cross those barriers and be all things to all people it is also essential to develop a schizophrenic musical personality, which the Supremes also did, as we shall see later.

Diana was not the Supreme who immediately caught the eye. True, she had come to be accepted by Motown as the most distinctive voice in the group and therefore the lead singer, and because of that most attention was fixed on her. But Mary Wilson was the most traditionally beautiful of the trio, while Florence Ballard's quiet and thoughtful demeanour gave the group a balancing, homely image.

Yet Diana was certainly different. A thin frame, large eyes – now staring, now hooded and sultry – and a wide red gash of a mouth full to overflowing with dazzlingly bright teeth. Once one's attention was caught, it was held firm. Her emergence as the focal point of the group was timely, for she had exactly the type of figure which the models of the sixties, from Jean Shrimpton to Twiggy, would popularize.

It was undoubtedly this *gamine* quality which had alerted Gordy to the commercial possibilities inherent in Diana's looks. She had a universal appeal to be more than just a singer in one of his groups using a lightly sexy, breathy style of delivery. He singled out her career and its development for close personal attention. She has often said that he was everything to her in those days: father, mother, sister, brother, lover. He had also told her not to worry about fears she had of not being pretty. Her face, he said, had 'character'.

Speculation about the prospect of Diana and Berry marrying each other persisted over many years, for it was the stuff of which gossip columnists' livelihoods are made, but came to nothing. For one thing Gordy was married (he has had three wives), but the relationship has nevertheless been long and strong and certainly affected the feelings of other women singers contracted to the label. Simply, they felt that while Diana Ross was working there they would not get the fullest possible attention from the writers and producers for more than a couple of singles. While the Supremes' records were hitting the top of the charts the popular group would get the best material. Hadn't *they* waited in line while Mary Wells and the Marvelettes were getting preference? What is unarguable is that Diana's singing with the Supremes helped define the label's particular sound and became a blueprint to which other artists adapted their work. Not every singer was as vocally pliable as Ross.

An early award (near right) for the Supremes' 'Where Did Our Love Go?' a number one hit in the United States and number three in Britain. Pop singer Mike Sarne (far right) was best known for a hit called 'Come Outside'. The Supremes think about the invitation. The only Supremes records not issued in Britain after August 1964 were the single 'Twinkle, Twinkle Little Me'/'Children's Christmas Song' and album Merry Christmas of 1965. The seasonal snap below shames such humbug

This was to be a boom time for the whole of the record industry. While the Detroit record company was refining its sound, a commercial upheaval was taking place in Britain with the equally speedy rise of the Beatles and, in their wake, the Mersey Sound followed by earthier bands of the 'white' rhythm and blues and beat boom. Any parallels drawn between the two events can only be tenuous. The Beatles helped to identify the existence of a new, large, post-war youth market of considerable affluence and eager for a new, more exciting sound. In the United States, Motown's developing soul music was providing the same sort of sustenance. By 1964, the Beatles and the British beat groups had begun to take their music to the USA in the first of many waves of a still continuing invasion, while in that same year the Motown Sound arrived in the mass market in Britain.

Motown had been known of, and its artists admired, almost from the very beginning. The Beatles played no small part in spreading the word by mentioning the artists and records in press interviews. John Lennon elected Marvin Gaye's 'Can I Get a Witness?' as a favourite single, George Harrison named Mary Wells as one of his favourite singers. On their second album, *With the Beatles*, they did versions of the Marvelettes' 'Please Mr Postman', Smokey Robinson's 'You Really Gotta Hold on Me' and of Berry Gordy's co-composition with Barrett Strong, 'Money'. Other British groups found the Motown catalogue an effective way to get into the charts. The Contours' 'Do You Love Me?' was good for both the Dave Clark Five and Brian Poole and the Tremeloes, and the latter group also did the Isley Brothers' 'Twist and Shout', which the Beatles included on their first album. And like 'Money', which became a hit for Bern Elliot and the Fenmen, 'Twist and Shout' became a standard item in the set of almost every British group of that time.

Conversely, the British beat boom had little effect on the music of Motown. How could it, really, when all that the British groups were doing was re-exporting American music back to the United States with a dash of youthful British verve and irreverence. Of course, Motown duly paid tributes such as the 1965 Supremes' album *With Love (from Us to You)*, which included hits by the Beatles, Gerry and the Pace-

34

makers, Cilla Black, the Animals and the Dave Clark Five. The irony suggested by the inclusion of versions of Motown's own 'You Really Gotta Hold on Me' and 'Do You Love Me?' highlighted the label's contribution to this British eruption.

After the impression made by 'When the Lovelight' and the hiccough that followed with 'Run, Run, Run', the Supremes went back into the studios to add their vocals to more Holland-Dozier-Holland songs. The group was impressed neither by the material offered them nor by the finished performances. Florence brooded, while Mary cried herself to sleep, and Diana certainly turned no cartwheels.

When the first single from the session was released the Supremes were out on the road. One could calculate the single's progress on the charts by the group's rise from bottom-of-the-bill to, only six weeks later, the headline attraction. The single was 'Where Did Our Love Go?'. It went to number one in the United States and three in Britain. It began a sequence of fifteen consecutive top twenty hits in America between July 1964 and December 1967, all of which were written by Holland-Dozier-Holland and produced by Dozier and Brian Holland.

'Where Did Our Love Go?', which had reached the top of the charts in the United States in just three weeks, set the pattern for Supremes singles thereafter. Mary and Florence were gradually reduced to contributing little more than 'oohs', 'aahs', various terms of endearment and confirmations of the song's title. On this first big hit their part amounts to 'baby, baby' and 'where did our love go?' This is not meant to decry their worth but to emphasize the fact that Gordy and his producers had already decided to throw the full weight of the songs and productions on to Diana's voice.

Diana's is by no means the most expressive or powerful voice in black music, yet its high pitch and slightly cutting, nasal tone, which frankly infuriated those of thin temper who found it piercing, were the very qualities which made it the perfect foil for Holland and Dozier's pop productions and the toppy sound they created. She could conjure a plaintive and fragile mood with ease and cope with an exultant melody, could certainly do justice to a pleading lyric, and when a song's delivery required defiance or

anger she managed to inject enough nastiness and venom into her otherwise rather thin tone to suggest that the object of her wrath was in for serious trouble.

On 'Where Did Our Love Go?' Diana wore, as it were, her plaintive hat. The song opens with the ominous sound of echoey, clomping feet. Holland and Dozier built the production carefully through the first two verses, bringing instruments gradually on top of the basic track of bass, piano, then drums, vibes, and background vocals. The clomping feet are the steps of Diana's lover on his way out. Her delivery of the lyric is something of a revelation in the light of what one would have expected after previous singles. In the space of a couple of minutes she has ruefully scolded the man for first hooking her and then attempting to cast her off, she has nostalgically reflected on their first meetings, and sounds puzzled and hurt at finding herself suddenly thrown over. Yet the mood of the finished song is far from desolate. The fast walking pace gives the track a sprightly atmosphere, which contrasts with the bleak lyric and makes the song danceable. Although they weren't as ingenious at writing lyrics as Smokey Robinson, Holland-Dozier-Holland were astute enough to hammer home the burden of a song's storyline, and if their metaphors were occasionally rather clumsily constructed and imagined, their meaning was impossible to misconstrue. Heartbreak was heartbreak, being in love was wonderful, and night-life was exciting.

The 'wholeness' of the Holland-Dozier-Holland productions from this time onwards, certainly for the next four years, was at the core of Motown's every effort now. They were complete *sounds*. Holland and Dozier never cluttered the Supremes' singles with instrumentation. They used what was readily available with immense skill and deftness, and the most insignificant touch, like the striking of a triangle or chime at a certain moment, would assume critical importance within the scope of a production and rivet the attention. They also used the ever-improving technology at the Motown studios imaginatively, and learned from the mistakes made by previous production teams who had less sophisticated recording equipment.

The Supremes' second single in this impressive sequence was 'Baby Love'. The production started by making reference to the first smash hit: prominent stomping feet – yes, Diana's lover is leaving again – added to tinkling piano, cymbal and bass drum. But when Diana's cooing 'Hoo-oooh' announces the main portion of the song, the emphatic beat gives way to a lighter, skippier rhythm beneath a more prominent contribution from Mary and Florence and the warmer, coaxing tone of Diana's lead pleading with the departing lover to stay. The way in which Holland and Dozier introduce the brief instrumental break is especially subtle, gently insinuating a tenor saxophone into the arrangement and allowing Diana's lead to cut off unexpectedly, leaving the background vocals to continue their refrain while the small horn section offers its version of the melody before Diana's lead returns. But one verse later the tenor sax again insinuates itself into the background to make further comments on the situation.

'Where Did Our Love Go?' and 'Baby Love' had displayed most of the facets of Diana's voice which made it perfect for pop music. There was a coy, sexual quality, a certain natural grace, a definite nasal tone occasionally brittle and harsh, and a sense of versatility in that this voice would be able to adapt to most pop settings in which it was placed. Although Motown's records would later become reviled for being repetitive and hackneyed, this is a glib generalization brought on by superficial consideration of the sound (a generalization which persists to this day when rock critics pontificate on black music).

Like their label-mate Smokey Robinson, Holland-Dozier-Holland did not stick to the pop norm of using a set sequence of verses and choruses broken by a middle eight. Perhaps less structurally adventurous than Robinson, the three writers still sprang surprises in arrangements and frequently challenged the singer with an unexpected chord change.

Once the Motown Sound was established, other producers who worked within it found their own way of expressing themselves, and it is absolutely undeniable that, say, Norman Whitfield or Smokey Robinson productions are clearly different from Holland-Dozier-Holland's, yet they all have the essence of the sixties' Motown Sound.

The composed graduates of Miss Powell's deportment classes. Whether 'informally' posed with the traditional British cuppa (far left) or contemplating an early autumn fall of leaves (second left), whether backstage (left) or onstage (below) the Supremes carried themselves stylishly. Diana and Mary supplied the glamour while Florence gave them a homely, shy but approachable touch

Quite how Holland-Dozier-Holland made such a *big* sound in such unprepossessing surroundings on equipment, though improving, still of a decidedly rudimentary nature, remains speculative. The musicians used in the studio simply shrug and say there were no secrets, that it was all attributable to the rooms used, be it the old back bedroom or, later, the basement.

Gordy and his producers were aware, too, of the fast expansion that the radio and record-player industries had undergone. The spread of transistorized radios and portable record-players, which depended on the development of small speakers, meant that certain frequencies sounded better over the radio or on the turntable. So Motown producers increased the treble on their records, fattened the bass as much as possible, added echo to both and left the grey, middle-register area alone. This emphasis on the top and bottom sound frequencies worked splendidly. No records sounded better, or were more immediately recognizable on transistor or Dansette player, than Motown's. They leapt out of the speakers.

The new small speakers also meant that more and more cars had built-in radios on their dashboards and Motown's sound, with its compulsive rhythm, was the perfect music to accompany a long drive on an inter-state freeway or, in Britain, a new motorway. And it had the right sort of hipness and uptown, night-time volatility to accompany a cruise round the streets – loud, crackly, atmospheric, ecstatic.

In Britain, the new generation of kids with money to spend were catered for by discotheques which sprang up in all of the main cities, using the rhythmic, danceable music of black America as its staple diet. 'Baby Love' was a number one hit on both sides of the Atlantic. In Britain it made the Supremes one of only two American artists to top the charts in 1964, so complete was the domination of home-grown talent.

After 'Baby Love', the Supremes' writers came up with 'Come See About Me'. Their third consecutive American number one, the single didn't make the top twenty in Britain, which was certainly a surprise after reaching positions three and one with the two previous singles. One reason for the failure in Britain was that the label which was distributing Motown in Britain, Stateside, was about to lose its client. 'Come See About Me' was released in Britain in January 1965, and in March of that year the Tamla Motown label was to start business in Britain under its own name in the distribution deal with EMI.

Stateside had also released the group's first album, *Meet the Supremes*, which was simply a collection of the A and B sides the group had issued on singles up to and including 'Where Did Our Love Go?' This makeweight attitude to LP work was to persist with the label for almost the whole of the sixties and was another reason why their work was taken less seriously by rock writers than might otherwise have been the case. Since the Beatles, albums have gradually increased in importance. They have offered good value and the artist could, assuming he or she had the wherewithal, be more creative. But Motown saw the LP, especially in the Supremes' case, as the repository for B sides, failed experiments and the recordings which indicated how the group would develop as a stage 'presentation'. As early as 1964 Mary Wilson, during their first UK trip, was admitting that 'our singing is for night clubs' and that their already cabaret-orientated act was 'very carefully worked out beforehand'. Contrasted with 'the Sound of Young America' which permeated their singles, this was a signpost to the musical schizophrenia to follow.

Indeed by 1968 Diana would be able to say that: 'We don't really need hit records now because we can work the night club and hotel circuit. As soon as we started making records we began putting a stage act together and as this developed it made us less dependent on hit records. We'd like to record more standards and we hope to. The reason we record so many Holland-Dozier-Holland songs is simply because they keep coming up with the best numbers.'

By 19 March 1965, when the first single on Tamla Motown in Britain was issued, the song was already at the top of the American charts. The Supremes' 'Stop in the Name of Love' was by far the most assertive and dramatic track the group had cut since 'When the Lovelight Starts Shining'. A swelling organ chord is interrupted by a commanding cry of 'Stop!' from the three women. The forceful four-four rhythm is immediately picked up by snare drum and tambourine.

It had been usual in pop for the snare drum to play the off-beats of a bar (that is, beats two and four of a four-four bar) and the bass drum to play the on-beats (that is, beats one and three). Now, however, Holland-Dozier-Holland spread the emphasis evenly across the bar, having the snare drum, boosted by tambourine, cracking out all four beats. This gave great thrust to the rhythm of the song. It also added to the top-heavy bias of the sound, again ideal for transistors, portables and jukeboxes. Additionally, as it was itself a gospel rhythmic style, the gospel intonations of the singing were nudged to the fore.

In 'Stop' the off-beat (or up-beat) was emphasized by electric guitar chording on beats two and four, leaving the bass end of the sound to the bass guitar. These hard sounds were cushioned by the use of electric organ and a gently chiming vibraphone. This contrast of hard and soft sounds matches the lyric's mood. Diana is again faced with the loss of her man; this time, however, she's surer of her worth, having put up with his affairs and treated him more than fairly. Think it over, she both pleads and warns, for you won't find another like me. It's one of Holland-Dozier-Holland's better lyrics and Diana sings it in a sweet, reasoning style as though she were explaining the workings of some complicated device to a child.

The Supremes had another three singles released in 1965 – 'Back in My Arms Again', 'Nothing but Heartaches' and 'I Hear a Symphony' – and only 'Heartaches' failed to get to the number one position in the United States. So in the period from July 1964 to December 1965 they had had six number one records in the USA out of seven releases, and during that time had been in the top twenty for fifty-one weeks.

In April 1965, just after the launch of Motown in Britain, the Supremes made their first tour of Britain (the previous trip had only been promotional) and the British press had a first glimpse of the protégées of the Motown grooming school at work. The interviews conducted were perfunctory and bland, the views on British music and customs politeness personified, and the performances oozed charm and grace of a rather deliberate sort. The lessons of glamour take time, and a certain maturity, to be absorbed and converted into performing currency.

The rising status of the Supremes had meant changes at Motown. When their contracts expired, women singers such as Mary Wells and Kim Weston left the label rather than remain in the shadow of Diana and be treated, in their opinion, like second-class citizens. But Motown was still the label that every hopeful black singer or musician aspired to join. Although commercial success was bringing strains and jealousies, the company, had not yet lost the tight-knit family feeling and sharing of a common, hit-making purpose. Gordy was well on the way to achieving his goal of huge commercial success and acceptance in the white pop market where he felt stability and respectability lay. The Supremes, his act most obviously suited to the cross-over, had developed two musical personalities, cultivating the youth market through their singles and on albums recording the songs they believed to be more adult and sophisticated.

These albums tended to have themes such as tributes (*We Remember Sam Cooke*) or homages to other styles (*With Love (from Us to You)* and *The Supremes Sing Country, Western and Pop*). But more and more the group were given white standards to sing, such as 'Stranger in Paradise', 'With a Song in My Heart', and 'Unchained Melody', and they were rarely produced on albums by Holland and Dozier. This was Gordy's strategy to make Diana and the Supremes acceptable on television nationwide, able to win an adult audience and to prove their readiness to move into the Las Vegas live show circuit, the Mecca for most American entertainers but anathema to the young kids from whom the Supremes got their first response. For a long while it seemed as though Motown didn't believe that fans who bought singles would buy albums too.

Another tour begins: the Supremes arrive at Heathrow (far left). All smiles as (top left, this page) Martha (centre) and the Vandellas push the Supremes towards Customs. In reality, however, many of the other women artists at Motown felt they'd always be treated second best while Diana was around. And (above) Diana's traffic-stopping dash across the road foretells the split to come

4. FAREWELL IS A LONELY SOUND

During the years 1965–7 the Supremes were one of only three groups consistently able to challenge the dominance of British beat groups in the American top ten. The others were the Beach Boys and the Four Seasons. In Britain, the Supremes' hits came less regularly at first and only achieved similar consistency from the autumn of 1966 onwards. For example, in the spring of 1965 'Stop in the Name of Love' reached the British top twenty, but none of the subsequent five singles was a hit until in September 1966 'You Can't Hurry Love' got to number three. By then the trio had already had two American hits in that year alone with 'My World Is Empty without You' (in February it reached fifth place on the charts) and 'Love Is Like an Itching in My Heart' (May, number nine).

'My World' is a fine example of Holland-Dozier-Holland's ability to create a precise mood in which Ross could work. Although taken at a pacy gallop, the echoey bass drum and rather funereal electric organ set a sombre tone which is immediately picked up by the bass guitar, gloomily chiming vibes and Ross's matter-of-fact statement of her predicament. Man gone, world ended. Cold, hard, miserable existence. Again, the producers build the cut masterfully, adding instruments in a sequence so natural that one hardly notices how full the sound becomes. Then a bare, brutally simple baritone sax break tops off a truly bleak record.

'Itching' is a more typical Motown Sound. On 'My World' Mary and Florence had hardly featured at all. Here, they are brought more into the picture, and although their contribution is still limited in content to 'oohs' and 'aahs', their extra comments and responses to Diana's lead do colour the vocal. Diana's voice again shifts character to become a tight-throated object of great frailty which now and then breaks out to emit an aggressive growl. The accompaniment distils most of what had by now become *the* Motown Sound. Relentless four-four rhythm on the snare drum is bolstered by tambourine on the off-beat, vibes, chimes or calliope fill the treble range, the hard, boomy bass drum and bass guitar occupy the lower range and tough horn playing shares the middle ground with the vocals. The tempo of 'Itching' is similar to Stevie Wonder's 'Uptight', which had

been a hit three months previously, but Ross's vocal is patently less exuberant than Wonder's.

The group's next single began a run of four consecutive number one pop hits in America, all of which went into the UK top twenty, three of them into the top ten. It was, in fact, another important period in the group's development.

Having evolved the distinctive Motown Sound that Berry Gordy sought – and one that was by now being imitated by very many black American soloists and groups – Holland-Dozier-Holland were always keen to experiment with the Sound and expand its scope in order to maintain its freshness and stay ahead of the mimics. In this they were aided by the expanding recording studio hardware industry which offered all manner of new gadgetry to help create bigger and clearer sound reproduction.

Such improvements were reflected on both sides of the Atlantic. Once the British record companies, agents, managers and groups had seen what rich pickings might be had on the other side of the pond, the industry in Britain grew at a tremendous rate, fuelled by the publicity about London, Carnaby Street and the swinging sixties. On record, the Beatles and producer George Martin led the way in Britain with the power and richness of sound on their singles during 1966–7 from 'Paperback Writer' through 'Penny Lane' to 'Strawberry Fields Forever', and the *Sergeant Pepper's Lonely Hearts Club Band* album and *Magical Mystery Tour* EP and LP.

In the United States, white rock bands on the West Coast were using the new technology to express the feelings and aspirations of a youth culture increasingly based on supposedly consciousness-expanding drugs. Gordy, with his desire for a mass audience and middle-American acceptance for his major stars, would have no truck with such associations. So the problem was, how to incorporate the new effects to best advantage? The label certainly was not keen to lose the basic sound that had been developed, but neither did Holland-Dozier-Holland wish to be left behind and seem old-fashioned. That times would catch up with them was inevitable. In pop music, a particular sound and style rarely enjoy consistent popularity for more than two or three years. By then the originators have been copied by less talented

artists or producers, and the uniqueness they once offered has disappeared. The sound becomes almost universal and reaches saturation point, and unless a new variation can quickly be evolved then a new sound will spring up to replace it. So rather than repeat the standard clichés about the decline of Motown's sound in the late sixties, it seems to me that, on recordings, the label tackled the changes as well as, indeed better than, most other contemporary black producers and groups. It was achieved through a mixture of compromise and innovation, most of which was the result of the efforts of new producers like Norman Whitfield, who carried on the work of Holland-Dozier-Holland. Diana Ross played only a peripheral role in these changes – she was still the label's 'cover girl', as it were, and for the most part strictly uncontroversial. But we have rather run ahead of the Diana Ross story.

The first of the four number one hits, 'You Can't Hurry Love', was one of the Supremes' more exultant vocal performances, with Mary and Florence given bigger supporting roles to play, echoing the supposed warnings of Ross's mother concerning the danger of haste in affairs of the heart. Frankly, after a succession of songs about Diana losing her man such a warning might seem superfluous.

Apart from the immense amount of top (guitar chords, drums, tambourine) sharing the upper register with Diana's echoey, free-sounding lead balanced only by a boomy bass guitar, the single is notable for Ross's phrasing. As well as giving one of her most assertive early singing performances, she shows confidence with the lyric and melody and seems to relish the freer role as lead singer, using a jazzier phrasing and intonation. Because this performance occurred in a pop single telling of a young girl's memory of her mother's advice, most critics ignored the comparative daring and skill applied by Diana to her delivery. But they certainly couldn't neglect the sheer vivacity of the performance.

That single was followed later in 1966 by 'You Keep Me Hangin' On', in which Diana and the Supremes returned to the bleaker pastures of 'My World Is Empty without You'. Here, however, the arrangement and production have greater drama. Held together by a morse code-like figure played on

guitar, the production places greater emphasis on the bottom register – the morse code figure replaced by rapped bongoes during verses and tambourine aside – building from a rock-solid bass guitar line to give Diana a strong platform on which to act out her desperate struggle to rid herself of her man, yet another in the succession of no-good cheats with whom Holland-Dozier-Holland put her in touch. Although he says their romance is over, he is unwilling finally to cut the thread which binds them. Diana's last, angry dismissal of him, demanding that he be a man and get out of her life for ever, is unequivocal.

'Love Is Here and Now You're Gone' (February) and 'The Happening' (April) started 1967 in the same form in which the Supremes had seen out 1966. The former single was most notable for Ross's spoken passages punctuating the broken arrangement, which tended to deflect attention from her strong singing, pulled yet further to the fore, and her producers' use of a powerful string section plus harpsichord-like phrases from the keyboard section. It's one of Holland and Dozier's productions that reveals more than one ever expects is there.

'The Happening', by contrast, suggests more than it actually possesses. Holland-Dozier-Holland wrote the song with Frank DeVol for an eponymous movie starring Anthony Quinn and Faye Dunaway. The film was considerably less successful than the single (number one in the United States, number six in Britain) but even the record, one suspects, rode on the coat-tails of the group's previous hits.

'The Happening', however, was a prophetic enough title for the Supremes as they approached that summer of 1967. Two things happened: Florence Ballard left the group in August and was replaced by Cindy Birdsong, and Aretha Franklin's 'Respect' reached number one in the United States in May, number ten in Britain in July.

The phenomenal success that Gordy had achieved with his labels since forming them in 1960 had alerted the rest of black American writers, musicians, producers and singers to the realization that sustained commercial success in the white market was possible. And pop-orientated soul music, the blend of rhythm and blues and gospel, had also whetted the appetites of the white market for more black music. But as we

Cindy Birdsong (far right) replaced Florence Ballard. Born on 15 December 1939, she was an ex-member of Patti LaBelle and the Bluebelles and fitted in perfectly with the ever-increasing Las Vegas bias of the group's act, as can be seen in this song shared with Sammy Davis Jr

have seen, the Supremes had been increasingly less committed to the white pop market, outside the quarterly release of a single. Albums and stage shows were middle-aged by comparison. They had become favourites on most of the American TV chat shows, making guest appearances on everything from the Ed Sullivan, Mike Douglas and Steve Allen shows to the Dean Martin and Sammy Davis Jr shows, from *The Red Skelton Hour* and *Hollywood Palace* to *The Johnny Carson Show* and specials such as *Rodgers and Hart Today*, as well as pop shows such as *Hullabaloo* and *Shindig*. They made novelty guest appearances in TV series like *Tarzan*, popped up in teen movies such as *Beach Party* and sang for films such as *Dr Goldfoot and the Bikini Machine*. They became regulars at the big Las Vegas clubs and hotel lounges. Their albums continued to be collections of their own hits, standards and other Motown acts' hits, all recorded as quickly as possible, with the minimum of agonizing, at stop-overs in Detroit during tours.

All this created an enormous distance between the group and its fans and into the gap stepped Aretha Franklin. Her earthier singing was precisely what the fans of black American music had come to miss in Motown's records as the pop sound of the company became increasingly more attuned to the mass market. At the same time the mass white market, through the raucous singing of the white rhythm and blues singers such as Eric Burdon with the Animals and Mick Jagger with the Rolling Stones, had become used to rougher vocals and were ripe for exposure to the genuine article.

After many years with CBS, Aretha Franklin had been signed to Atlantic Records and taken down to Muscle Shoals in Alabama by producer Jerry Wexler who simply set her loose on a series of powerful ballads and thrilling up-tempo arrangements. Her vibrant, gospel-trained voice, and the strength of conviction with which she delivered herself, suddenly made the Supremes' hits like 'The Happening' sound utterly trite.

Other black-dominated record companies which had followed in Motown's wake began to exert an influence on the pop market. Stax of Memphis, through their subsidiary, Volt, and Otis Redding, who became the face and voice of popular soul in the

The old (far left, top) and the new (bottom) Supremes look. The accessible, girl-next-door look of Florence and Mary has gone and the glamorous look that was developed in Diana is transferred to Cindy and Mary, a group image that's all shimmer and sequins with Mary quite obviously relishing it. Meanwhile (near left) Berry Gordy and Diana, attending the Hollywood premiere of Funny Girl, chat to the movie's producer, Ray Stark. Gordy eyes Stark in much the same way as he was eyeing the movie industry in general – eagerly

late sixties as the base for black American music swung from the northern industrial cities to the southern states.

Motown seemed content to let this go on while they pursued their quest for an ever-wider market. They tried to cling on to part of the new market for a more virile approach to rhythm and blues by setting up the Soul label and signing artists such as Gladys Knight and the Pips, whose style fell somewhere between the passion of Aretha and the glamour of Diana. For a while the investment was repaid, but eventually Knight too became disgruntled at the label's insistence that Diana Ross and the label's other major acts would always receive preferential treatment; so, like others before and since, she went elsewhere to be a white-dominated label's number one black act.

Gordy's favouritism in guiding Ross's career aside, it should be noted that those who left Motown and put themselves on the open market were usually in great demand by white labels simply because of what they had achieved with Motown. And surprisingly few of the acts ever improved on the artistic and commercial success they had had at Motown, which speaks volumes for the skill of the writers, producers and musicians involved. But it remains undeniable that dissatisfaction among the less established Motown artists was frequent.

As to the change which specifically affected the Supremes in the summer of 1967, rumours about the future of Florence Ballard began to circulate when she missed a concert at the Hollywood Bowl. Soon afterwards the split was confirmed. Initially, the statement was that Florence had tired of the touring and travelling involved in being a Supreme and wanted to settle down and spend more time with her family. Then it was learned that she had had a virus and had been in hospital, but would be embarking on a solo career. She signed a contract with ABC Records and released a few George Kerr-produced singles, such as 'It Doesn't Matter How I Say It (It's What I Say)', but they did nothing. She suffered nervous breakdowns, sadly faded from the music scene, was heard of working as a maid and only resurfaced in the seventies in the most tragic of circumstances.

Florence's replacement, Cindy Birdsong, had deputized for her at the Hollywood Bowl concert. Cindy had been a member of the Bluebelles, who had had a hit as far back as 1962 with 'I Sold My Heart to the Junkman' and who later became known as Patti Labelle and the Bluebelles. They had further hits with 'Down the Aisle (Wedding Song)' and were known for rather melodramatic versions of standards such as 'Danny Boy' and 'Over the Rainbow'. Such experience singled Cindy out as the ideal replacement for the unfortunate Ballard because she would obviously be at home with the group's live material and on albums like Sing Rodgers and Hart and Sing and Perform Funny Girl.

A third and final change at this time was perhaps the most significant in regard to Diana's story. The Supremes were henceforth to be known as Diana Ross and the Supremes. Two similar alterations in name at Motown brought other lead singers to the fore. The Miracles became Smokey Robinson and the Miracles and Martha and the Vandellas became Martha Reeves and the Vandellas. In all three cases the move was a prelude to the final severing of lead singer from background vocalists.

But Diana Ross and the Supremes had another two-and-a-half years' hit-making to go yet. The first single by the new line-up was Holland-Dozier-Holland's 'Reflections'. The producers took the morse code effect of 'Love Is Here' and transformed it into electronic bleeps which fade into the distance like dying echoes. More interesting than this effect was the closeness with which the tempo, socking four-four snare drum beat, string arrangement, background vocals, use of woodwinds and the swelling arrangement followed the pattern used by the producers a year earlier on the Four Tops' 'Reach Out I'll Be There'. That record, a number one hit on both sides of the Atlantic, was the single which, in 1966, finally opened the floodgates to total acceptance of Motown's hits in Britain.

'Reflections' was another enjoyable instance of Holland-Dozier-Holland recycling their work to good artistic and commercial profit. The Supremes' single got to number two in the United States and five in Britain. Their last single of 1977, 'In and Out of Love', was a rather ordinary song with little of that careful construction and imagination which had distinguished most of the previous collaborations between the group and its writers/producers. A jolly mood and danceable tempo are about all that can be said in its favour.

The next single, 'Forever Came Today', didn't even make the top twenty. It was the group's first single to fail in the United States for three-and-a-half years. In fact, the single was a year old when it was released. The beginning of 1968 was certainly a critical time for Diana Ross and the Supremes.

There were fundamental problems at Motown. Not only were several of the artists demanding more attention and better material, but now Holland-Dozier-Holland, whose importance to the label in the mid-sixties growth period cannot be over-estimated, decided to quit the corporation and set up their own labels, Invictus and Hot Wax. When they settled the legal battle with Motown which followed their departure, the writer/producers had some early successes with Chairmen of the Board, Freda Payne and Honey Cone, but the hit-rate wasn't maintained and the partnership broke up in the seventies. Lamont Dozier became a solo recording star of some repute and the Holland brothers have latterly returned to freelance production work.

Without the team who had shown they knew Ross's qualities as a singer so well, it seemed that Gordy had been far-sighted by ensuring that the trio had, by 1968, become a bill-topping, house-filling cabaret attraction. That year, for instance, the group made its last trips to the United Kingdom with Diana as lead vocalist. A live album of their February performance at the Talk of the Town in London was fairly representative of the type of act they put out in those days: a medley of standards such as 'With a Song in My Heart', 'Stranger in Paradise', 'Wonderful, Wonderful' and 'Without a Song'; a medley of early hits; a résumé of their latest releases; movie and show tunes like 'Mame', 'Thoroughly Modern Millie' and 'Second-hand Rose' . . . a mixture which would hardly satisfy the majority of their very first fans but one that was manna to those who went along for the glamour, the spectacle of shiny evening gowns, bouffant wigs and glistening smiles.

Remarkably, by the time the group returned in November of that year for a tour and appearance at the Royal Variety Performance at the London Palladium, they were back at the top of the American charts with, of all things, a single that had the scent of controversy about it. Black America was becoming politicized. The rather bland comments of Motown artists, including Diana Ross and the Supremes, were beginning to sound soft-centred, empty, and Uncle Tom beside the contentious remarks of black civil rights leaders and their more militant brothers in the Panthers – just as the music, though unquestionably bigger-sounding than before, seemed less and less relevant to the angrier mood of the young blacks. Although the company had by now become so establishment that it would never be able to represent the black radicals, even if Gordy wanted it to, Motown demonstrably needed new blood, younger blood, in the writing and production of tracks. The departure of Holland-Dozier-Holland presented them with no option but to revitalize those areas.

One of the results of the recruitments that followed was the signing of the team of Nicholas Ashford and Valerie Simpson, who'd built a good reputation as writers on tunes such as 'Let's Go Get Stoned' for Ray Charles. They were put with Diana Ross and the Supremes and on the first single, 'Some Things You Never Get Used To', they showed the quirky touch for instrumentation which Holland-Dozier-Holland had by using castanets during the introduction and referring to them throughout the track. Their melody line was more flexible than most of their predecessors', which tended to be less rangy. But the playing on 'Some Things' was stiff and the arrangement over-deliberate, and Diana's voice had to manoeuvre dexterously through this stilted, unbending background. The single sold poorly by comparison with the Holland-Dozier-Holland hits.

But then several of the new writers at Motown came up with a theme stronger than just falling in or out of love or being mistreated by one swine or another. Pam Sawyer, R. Dean Taylor, Frank Wilson and Deke Richards co-wrote 'Love Child'. The song's lyric told about an illegitimate child brought up in the ghetto, the stigma attached to bastard children, the poverty of the environment, the grim emotional start in life and the well of affection the child was

waiting to offer the first person to show it any love. For Motown, and pop music in 1968, this was a substantially stronger statement about social conditions and morals than was usual, a fact which critics of Diana Ross and the Supremes tend to ignore. When 'Love Child' was at number one in the United States, the British record buyers had placed Hugo Montenegro's version of the film theme 'The Good, the Bad and the Ugly' and Scaffold's novelty record 'Lily the Pink' in that exalted position in Britain. 'Love Child' eventually reached the British top twenty in Britain in December 1968, but never rose higher than fifteenth place.

The song had been produced by Gordy, Henry Cosby and three of its composers, Wilson, Richards and Taylor. The arrangement made the most of the song's drama and passion but also returned to earlier production values which had been superseded in the past twelve months. They simply unpacked the tambourines again and gave the cut's treble a massive boost; swooping violins, maraccas, snappy snare drum and underneath, bass guitar and brooding violas and cellos. Diana's vocal is pitched higher and has to reach for the notes with a shade more desperation, to bring out the anguish of the lyrics. After the first verse her singing also has a toppy sibilance which reinforces the edgy tone and feel of the single.

The controversy didn't stop with that song's lyrics. During the trio's appearance at the Royal Command Performance, attended by the Queen Mother, Prince Charles, Princess Anne, Princess Margaret and Lord Snowdon, Diana dedicated the performance of 'Somewhere', as she had been doing in the United States since the event, to the then recently assassinated Dr Martin Luther King, the black civil rights leader. That dedication became front page news in all the daily papers.

Although this was pretty mild stuff compared to what might have been, and was being, said, it was a further indication of how Motown was trying to adjust, through its acts, to the new black feeling in America. That the comment was made in front of members of the royal family was reason enough to excite the British press. That the comment was made by one of the by now most glamorous stars of

53

Although the personnel had changed, the teaming of the Primes (Temptations) with their old sister group the Primettes (Diana Ross and the Supremes) proved inspired, with hits in 1968-9 on both sides of the Atlantic as well as successful TV spectaculars (far right). The Temptations (near right) are, from left, Paul Williams, Melvin Franklin, Eddie Kendricks, Otis Williams, and Dennis Edwards

showbusiness, who had never before shown the least inclination to express publicly what she might be feeling, was equally exceptional.

In the interviews which followed, Diana continued to be about as forthright as she – or any Motown artist at that time – had been. When asked by *Melody Maker* about the Black Power movement she said: 'I won't ever put down Stokely Carmichael because he had such a good philosophy. If it wasn't for people like him, things wouldn't be happening today. I think the militants have their place because you need someone to be strong.

'I know lots of militants and peaceful people and I admire them and understand them. I share the same feelings as James Brown when he says "I'm black and I'm proud." Why should my younger brother watch TV programmes and be made to think he's different just because he has kinky hair and because he hasn't got a pointed nose? He's just as beautiful, so why should he be made to feel different?'

An irony of the Command Performance was that Diana and the Supremes appeared on the same bill as the Black and White Ministrels, a British re-creation of the old American shows in which white singers blacked up to impersonate negroes, a type of act which the vast majority of American blacks found wholly insulting. Diana said: 'It brings back memories of sadness for the coloured people, although I don't dislike the act itself.' Here she was rather more keen to walk the tightrope between admission of affront and the politeness taught her by the grooming department.

But in case anyone should run away with the notion that Diana had suddenly become clench-fisted on stage, people were quickly disabused of such ideas by Motown's folksy pairing of the trio with the Temptations. The intention, of course, was to reunite the groups that had started out together almost ten years before – the Temptations as the Primes and Diana Ross and the Supremes as the Primettes. On singles, the pairing worked excellently. First, producers Frank Wilson and Nick Ashford took a 1966 Dee Dee Warwicke hit, written by Kenny Gamble and Jerry Ross, titled 'I'm Gonna Make You Love Me'. By using the lead voices of Diana and the Temptations' Eddie Kendricks, they

turned the song into a fulsome love duet. The single went to three in Britain and two in the United States in the winter of 1968–9.

The collaborations eventually included TV specials, with the zappy dance routines of the Temptations contrasting with the glamour of the Supremes, and three albums. In 1969 the two groups had two American rhythm and blues hits, together with remakes of Smokey Robinson's 'I'll Try Something New' and of Robbie Robertson of The Band's 'The Weight'. In Britain, Robinson's 'I Second That Emotion' reached the top twenty as a Temptations/Supremes duet.

Back on their own, Diana and the Supremes still contrasted their expensive clothes and lavish stage presentations with songs of poverty and desolation. From the same team who wrote 'Love Child' (though minus Deke Richards and with Gordy and Henry Cosby added), the group got 'I'm Livin' in Shame'. The 'shame' of illegitimacy was now replaced by an all too believable tale of a young girl growing up in poverty, being put through college by her hard-working, self-sacrificing mother, moving into a richer circle of friends, marrying wealth and living in fear that her new intimates would discover her real roots. Her mother dies in squalor without seeing her grandchildren, or daughter, hence her child's shame. This standard 'from the gutter to wealth but at what price?' story-line, like something out of a Harold Robbins or Sidney Sheldon potboiler novel, was quite well realized on record and the production (Gordy, Wilson, Cosby, Richards, Taylor), like that of 'Love Child', is both rich and toppy, giving the single a live, exciting feel.

'Shame' gave the group another hit on both sides of the Atlantic (it reached tenth place in the United States in February 1969, fourteenth in Britain in May), and although number one records were no longer automatic it seemed that the group had turned the corner after the slump which followed the loss of Holland-Dozier-Holland.

But long-term predictions were overshadowed by another wave of strong rumours from the United States that at last Diana was to leave the Supremes. The official announcement was made in October 1969, by which time Diana's replacement had been

rehearsing with Mary and Cindy for six months. Before embarking on the obligatory farewell tour, the group released two singles – 'The Composer' written and produced by Smokey Robinson, and Gordy/ Cosby's 'No Matter What Sign You Are', both of which were small hits in the USA. The final group hit with Diana was produced by Johnny Bristol and written by him with Harvey Fuqua and Jackie Beavers. If ever a song was tailored to wrench the last ounce of nostalgia from the occasion of a ten-year-old group losing its lead singer, it was 'Someday We'll Be Together'.

It opens with a reflective, mellow guitar figure in front of sweeping strings, and Mary and Cindy sing the title refrain farther forward in the mix than for a long, long time. Diana sings the first verses in an undemonstrative style and Bristol puts in his own brief shouts of encouragement. The vocal background is by far the most overtly gospel-influenced they had ever devised, with tingling call-and-response singing. The arrangement steadily raises the volume and emotional temperature to a shivering crescendo. No wonder the song brought the house down on every night of the farewell tour.

The final performance of Diana Ross and the Supremes took place on 14 January 1970 at the Frontier Hotel in Las Vegas. The performance was recorded and released as a double album and the last single went to number one in the United States in November 1969, and was still at number thirteen the following January. The tracks which remained in the can went on to an album titled *Cream of the Crop*, released in February 1970. And, repackaged albums and reissued singles apart, that was the end of Diana Ross and the Supremes, the most successful hit-making group of women in the sixties.

Before continuing with Diana's story, a brief diversion to see what happened to the rest of the group without her is not out of place. Diana was succeeded by Jean Terrell, sister of the heavyweight boxer Ernie, and the new trio, despite prophecies of doom, got off to a cracking start with six hits in 1970-2 ('Up the Ladder to the Roof', 'Stoned Love', 'Nathan Jones', 'Floy Joy', 'Automatically Sunshine' and, with the Four Tops, 'River Deep Mountain High').

However, as soon as Diana's career began to accelerate again the Supremes seemed to encounter the same problems that had afflicted other women singers at Motown in the sixties. They were shunted from producer to producer with little consistent attention, poor songs and a general feeling of disinterest in the group. In 1972 Cindy Birdsong married and left the group and was replaced by Lynda Lawrence. In 1973 Lynda left with Jean Terrell and their places were taken by Scherrie Payne (sister of Freda Payne, who had a big hit with 'Band of Gold' on Holland-Dozier-Holland's label Invictus) and the prodigal Cindy Birdsong. Then Cindy left again and was replaced by Susaye Green and finally the group split up entirely – again after the obligatory, tearful farewell tour – when Mary Wilson left in 1977 to start a solo career. She was, however, soon back in Britain with a billing which mentioned the word 'Supremes' but, due to contractual details, could not actually say outright that the group *was* the Supremes. The group included two other black singers whose most distinguishing feature was that they were both named Karen.

After a long series of farewell concerts (far left) Diana finally said goodbye to Mary and Cindy with the 1969 hit 'Someday We'll Be Together'. Last show was on 14 January 1970 in Las Vegas. Mary led several versions of the Supremes thereafter. The one shown above is Lynda Lawrence, Mary and Jean Terrell from 1972-3

5. HOW SWEET IT IS

Diana Ross was not the only Motown artist for whom the late sixties and early seventies was time for a fundamental change in career. Others, like Stevie Wonder and Marvin Gaye, went through radical reassessments of their musical ideas and business arrangements and the results were to affect all Motown artists, Diana included.

Stevie Wonder had come of age and the monies which had been invested for him during his teens now gave him a measure of economic independence. He announced his intention to leave Motown for another label at the expiration of his current contract, but in the event renegotiated with the help of an astute business manager and lawyer, Johanen Vigoda, and emerged with complete artistic control over everything he recorded. Motown effectively became his record manufacturer and distributor and had no creative say in his work.

This was a significant turnabout. Most of the acts until that time had worked at the beck and call of the producers and writers. The vocalists would go into the studio, listen to the completed track, which usually had a guide vocal often provided by the writer or producer, and then sing his, her or their part, sticking fairly closely to the guide vocal. Obviously, the more experienced the singer, the more he or she was allowed to express a lyric in their own way. But certainly Diana, for one, had become comfortable through the years with this method of working.

With his *Where I'm Coming From* album Wonder began a series of LPs conceived as projects rather than mere collections of possible singles plus fillers. Yet the catchy pop melodies in which he couched many of the songs, or the romping rhythms to which they were sung, ensured a flow of hits from the albums. More importantly, the albums (*Talking Book, Innervisions, Fulfillingness' First Finale*) all sold well and Wonder became a major rock star from the soul base.

Several other artists at Motown began to approach album recording in a similar vein. Marvin Gaye, always something of a maverick at the label, had for many months been in a state of hibernation since the death in 1970 of Tammi Terrell, with whom he had recorded several excellent duet singles, ('Ain't No Mountain High Enough', 'Ain't Nothing Like the Real Thing', 'You're All I Need to Get By', 'The Onion Song'). He re-emerged triumphant with a powerful, thoughtful album, *What's Goin' On*, which talked about social, environmental and political questions rather than just the affairs of the heart and body with which he'd previously been almost totally preoccupied.

Established artists at the company weren't alone in attempting to grasp pricklier nettles when writing new material. After the departure of Holland-Dozier-Holland in 1968, the Motown Sound had been gradually reshaped by producer Norman Whitfield, whose dramatic, drawn-out and richly ornamented, powerhouse productions with the Temptations and Undisputed Truth took the 'standard' Motown Sound away from the toppy productions of the mid-sixties, which had begun to sound tinny.

Whitfield's sound had more bottom and was earthier, and the singing was generally tougher to match his socially concerned lyrics. His hits with the Temptations ('Runaway Child, Running Wild', 'Don't Let the Joneses Get You Down', 'Psychedelic Shack', 'Ball of Confusion') were prime examples. Yet he could also turn in beautifully constructed and observed ballads with the group, such as 'I Wish It Would Rain' and 'Just My Imagination (Running Away with Me)'. He'd even contrived to marry the two styles brilliantly on album tracks such as the murky, ominous 'Smiling Faces Sometimes'.

Despite these progressive changes on the creative side of the corporation's activities, doubts existed about Motown in the seventies. In the late sixties Gordy had begun to move their entire operation away from its Detroit base to Los Angeles, where the record industry was becoming more and more concentrated. In business and climatic terms it was a logical move. But it further highlighted the fact that this was no longer a family company close to its artists in every possible way and in which everyone shared a common purpose. The desire to make hit records remained, of course, but the sense of oneness was gradually eroded as familiar names and faces faded from the picture. The business's turnover and roster, it seemed, had become so large that it could sustain very close contact with only a few of its

In addition to making hits for Motown, Diana also proved an adept talent scout when she recommended the Jackson Five (far right) from Gary, Indiana, whose hits made the label 'The Sound of Young America' once again. Right: Diana attends a Hollywood social function with Michael Jackson in the summer of 1973

artists. In addition, Gordy was constantly looking for ways to diversify his business base to maintain his move into white showbusiness markets. The move to California obviously facilitated Motown's entry into films.

While its established acts orientated themselves towards the new, important and profitable album market or split into solo singer and group, it was still noticeable that the label hadn't broken a new act for some while – and new talent is the lifeblood of any record label, big or small. Without it, the label stagnates. Motown's artists were all now in their mid-twenties or older – Wonder was the exception, but he'd been there so long that he too seemed very adult – and their audience had grown old with them. Younger, hipper bands who didn't dress in ruff-fronted shirts and flashy suits, who didn't do snappy, synchronized dance steps, had been blending rock with gospel-tinged soul and had been drawing white rock audiences. The best-known, and first, of these bands was Sly and the Family Stone. Norman Whitfield's productions were up to a point reflecting this change, but the new bands were self-contained – they played their own instruments as well as singing their own songs.

In 1967 a group of kids in Gary, Indiana had been brought to the attention of Diana. She strongly recommended them to Gordy and he duly signed them. The label spent time recording and grooming the group. The Jackson Five was launched in 1969 and for Motown it was like 1964 all over again. The group's first four singles went to number one in the USA in less than a year, and Motown was suddenly 'the Sound of Young America' again. The group combined the garish, peacock clothes of the new bands with old-style dance steps, played their own instruments with increasing assurance, and won the label a completely new teeny-bopper audience.

Meanwhile, Diana's solo career had been set in motion. Her move away from the Supremes had been presaged in 1969 when she appeared without them on a Dinah Shore TV special in the United States with Lucille Ball and Rowan and Martin, a comedy team whose *Laugh-In* show was popular on TV. The success of her guest spot on the show was an extra spur to go it alone.

After the final concert with the Supremes in January 1970, the rest of the year was spent preparing her recording and live debuts. She was put with writers/producers Nick Ashford and Valerie Simpson and the first single was released in the summer of that year. 'Reach Out and Touch (Somebody's Hand)' scraped into the American top twenty and didn't even make the top thirty in Britain; not an auspicious start. Strangely enough, the song stayed in her act throughout the decade and its message of fellowship and comfort gave her endless opportunities on stage to create that artificial closeness between audience and star by which the glamorous actually manage to reaffirm their distance.

When she took her solo act on the road the atmosphere was, as she said, of a 'let's see if Diana Ross can make it on her own show' nature. In the event, little had been left to chance. It had showbiz spectacle, exotic costumes (lots of them too – eight changes in a twenty-song programme), thorough attention to sound (a twenty-five-piece orchestra plus three background singers, the Blackberries) and lavish presentation including a couple of extra dancers and comedy routines. In all, it was a $60,000 package to razzle and dazzle. In New York in September 1970 the show sold out the 800-seat Waldorf Astoria for three weeks, and the glowing reviews in the American trade magazines and popular press dispelled any doubts about a slump in popularity with the cabaret and hotel lounge audience she had won in the late sixties.

Her first solo album, *Diana Ross*, had been released in the United States in May, just prior to her stage debut. In Britain it was held back for the Christmas market. It had been produced by Ashford and Simpson and had ten of their own songs plus a Johnny Bristol/Harvey Fuqua song, 'These Things Will Keep Me Loving You', which recalled her final number one hit with the Supremes, 'Someday We'll Be Together', which Bristol and Fuqua had produced.

Diana Ross showed what thought had gone into her solo move, how her prospective audience was seen and the way in which Gordy thought her sound should grow. The first side of the album has the Bristol/Fuqua connection with her past sound plus a couple of songs which had been Ashford/Simpson-

penned hits for Marvin Gaye and Tammi Terrell ('You're All I Need to Get By' and 'Ain't No Mountain High Enough'). It's a predominantly pop-orientated side.

On the album's second side, the producers used a mixture of rather more sombre lyrics, and the instrumentation and arrangements gave two-thirds of the tracks a darker, more desperate mood. There was a greater effort to adopt the sort of stance an album was now meant to take. For Ross, especially, this was something new. From the stagey drama of a song like 'Ain't No Mountain' on the first side to the grimmer drama of 'Keep an Eye' and 'Dark Side of the World' was a noticeable step. And the effusive orchestrations used on the tracks gave Diana the sort of large canvas settings she was coming to relish.

When it came to packaging the album, Motown and Diana tried to stress the more serious side of the songs' content. Diana was photographed dressed in an unironed white tee-shirt and cut-off jeans, sitting on the floor of a studio against a sepia backcloth. Her hair had been cut to a boyish length and she was gazing up at an unseen object off to her left. In her thin right arm was an apple. To some, this pose had been deliberately chosen to use the image of poverty as widely seen on famine relief posters and was, as such, a tasteless piece of marketing. Certainly it provided a sharp contrast with the image the company had always shown of Diana as the world's most glamorous black star, the inaccessible and untouchable dream girl.

After the 'Reach Out' single, Motown released 'Ain't No Mountain High Enough' in the late summer of 1970 and it set the seal on the Ross solo career, rocketing to number one in the USA and reaching number six in Britain. It was no surprise that the record sold so well, for its blend of piercing crescendoes and huskily spoken sections produced a melodramatic *tour de force*. On the one hand it verged on deliberate over-production, but those moments when the song came to a virtual standstill as though gathering breath for another crashing assault on the high-pitched refrain were truly exciting, tingling with expectation. The arrangement manipulates the listener's responses thoroughly.

By the end of the year Diana had a third solo single out in the United States as well as a second album. Both were held back in Britain until the spring of 1971. The single, another Ashford and Simpson song and production, but one which hadn't been included on the debut album, was 'Remember Me'. Like 'Mountain', it built from soft and gentle reflective moments to climactic peaks when Diana is joined by a keening group of gospel singers. The shimmering string section and a hyperactive bass guitarist colour and drive the arrangement. By way of change, the single did better in Britain, where it reached seventh position, than it did in the USA (sixteenth) and was a signpost to the future, for Diana would continue to increase her popularity in Britain – often in spite of changes taking place elsewhere in the UK music scene.

She increasingly moved into the world of big business spectaculars without the leavening of Holland-Dozier-Holland's singles to appeal on a constant basis to the teenage market in America, which by now had wholly embraced the Jackson Five. The new black market was also discovering an ever-growing number of hard-playing, self-contained bands blending James Brown-derived funk with rock and jazz – Kool and the Gang, Ohio Players, Earth, Wind and Fire, Parliament and Funkadelic.

But Gordy, through Ashford and Simpson and subsequent producers, saw Diana as a respectable album artist whose records ought now to be more representative of what she was as 'a star' and of what she was on stage, which was spectacular and glamorous. So despite early and occasional flirtations with material of a slightly more aware nature, her best was generally saved for love songs of a positive, optimistic type. In taking this path Gordy had identified the route that more and more black artists, writers and producers would take throughout the seventies. For after the socially aware and angry lyrics and sounds at the turn of the decade, the whole bias of black music in America steadily shifted towards optimism and positive thought as the black middle class expanded. Quite where this left the black poor, whose predicament had not changed and was now without voice, is debatable, though perhaps it repeated the aphorism that in a time of hardship and depression, escapism will thrive.

For her second solo album, *Everything Is Everything*, Diana left Ashford and Simpson and was placed with Deke Richards and Hal Davis; Richards had already worked with her in the late sixties as co-writer and co-producer on Supremes' hits. *Everything* was partly a reversion to the bad old days when the Supremes' albums were jumbled collections of hits and anything else that seemed like a good idea at the time. Apart from two tracks that were to become hit singles, both written by Richards, the album is weighed down with mediocre fillers from the Motown staff, versions of two Beatles songs, one Aretha Franklin tune (brave, if ultimately a mistake) and a version of a Carpenters hit. Even the album sleeve's picture of Ross in a modestly bejewelled little fish-net jump-suit number seemed to suggest that all that glistered was indeed not gold. But an event somewhat more momentous than a mere solo album was just around the corner. *Everything Is Everything* came out in the USA in October 1970. Three months later Diana married.

During the sixties there had been continuing rumours that Diana would eventually marry Berry Gordy. When, towards the end of the decade, he had assumed personal responsibility for her career, it seemed even more inevitable. So when she married Robert Silberstein in Las Vegas on 21 January 1971 the sense of shock was considerable, to say the least.

Silberstein, who in a business capacity was also known as Robert Ellis, was a Los Angeles public relations man who would at one time or another handle the affairs of artists such as Billy Preston and Chaka Khan. Showbusiness marriages are, of course, notoriously unstable and all the more so when both partners are heavily involved in demanding careers. Sacrifice on both sides is necessary and the external pressures exerted on the partnership can be extreme. At the time of the marriage Silberstein was twenty-five, Diana a few months away from her twenty-seventh birthday. The couple started a family straight away. The first of their three daughters, Rhonda Suzanne, was born on 14 August 1971. Between her marriage and that birth a ninety-minute TV special devoted to Diana had been recorded and was screened on 18 April on American TV. In it, Diana presented her 'discoveries', the Jackson Five, along with black

Sketches in TV spectaculars, such as the one with American comedian Bill Cosby (near right), built Diana's confidence for tackling larger film roles. Centre: Arriving at the London premiere of Lady Sings The Blues, *her first film, in Shaftesbury Avenue, 4 April 1973. Far right: Flowers after the first night*

comedian Bill Cosby and Danny Thomas, as well as singing hits and standards, appearing in several skits and doing impersonations of comedians such as Charlie Chaplin, W.C. Fields and Harpo Marx. She had become the traditional 'all-round entertainer' as envisaged by Gordy. She was presented by top showbiz names, her costumes were designed by top fashion names, and she was choreographed by the best on Broadway.

During the year she was voted Number One Female Vocalist by *Billboard*, the American trade magazine, and by the readers of the *New Musical Express*, the British pop weekly. After being named 1970 Entertainer of the Year by the National Association for the Advancement of Coloured People (NAACP), she became the 1971 Honorary Chairwoman of the Image Awards Presentation and at the 1971 gala won the Best TV Special of the Year award for the *Diana!* show. (Though just how many TV specials 'coloured people' had in America in 1971 is a moot point.)

A soundtrack album from the TV special was released in the United States in March 1971; *Everything Is Everything* came out in Britain in April. The soundtrack LP appeared in Britain in November 1971, by which time another studio album, *Surrender*, was on the racks in the USA. During the year she had also released singles such as a remake of the Four Tops' hit 'Reach Out I'll Be There', which failed to make the pop top twenty but reached seventeenth on the rhythm and blues charts. That track was released in Britain only as the B side of 'I'm Still Waiting' in the summer of 1971, which went to the top of the UK charts. Its follow-up, 'Surrender', reached the British top ten that winter. Neither single made the American top twenty and although 'Surrender' reached the rhythm and blues top twenty, 'I'm Still Waiting' only moved up as far as forty.

By so successfully wooing the cabaret, TV and middle-of-the-road (MOR) album audience, Diana had now lost touch with the youth market in America. In Britain, where prolonged absence had increased the appetite of her loyal fans, where the MOR market could put records on to the pop charts and where the new trends in black music had yet to take a firm hold, Diana's popularity remained high. The

British album *I'm Still Waiting* had been released a month after the TV soundtrack album, which enabled Motown to align the release schedules of the two countries more closely, although there would usually be a one- or two-month gap in releases.

The *I'm Still Waiting* album found Diana reunited with producers/writers Ashford and Simpson, although its title track was written by Deke Richards. The 'Remember Me' hit from 1970–1, her long version of 'Reach Out' and a treatment of 'Didn't You Know (You'd Have to Cry Sometime)', which the producers had first done with Gladys Knight and the Pips, were included on the album. Like most of Diana's work with Ashford and Simpson, the album had some fine moments, mostly because of the producers' grasp of the need to infuse the background vocals with a high degree of gospel power. Arranger Paul Riser provided a set of subtly theatrical settings using increasingly larger string and horn sections. Ashford and Simpson were striving to strike a balance between the artist's Vegas tradition of show-stopping tunes in blockbusting arrangements and the maintenance of some small hold on her, and their, gospel roots. *I'm Still Waiting* was, however, the last album for several years on which such care and attention was to be lavished, for Gordy had other plans for his top woman artist.

During the whole of 1972 Diana released no records in the United States. In Britain, Motown lifted one single off her *Everything Is Everything* album, the ponderously tilted 'Doobedood'ndoobe, Doobedood'ndoobe, Doobedood'ndoo', a fairly daft, fairly catchy song written by Deke Richards, probably with a view to causing maximum embarrassment to DJs. Released in April 1972, it managed twelfth place in the UK charts. Diana's absence from the recording scene was simply explained. She was immersed in her role as Billie Holiday in *Lady Sings the Blues*.

The film, which began shooting in December 1971, was the next part in Gordy's game-plan to elevate Diana Ross to the position of international superstar. There was a cliché which any budding family entertainer of the fifties and early sixties was encouraged to mouth in order to break out of the pop music market. It was that he or she had one

ambition: to become a star of 'stage, screen and radio'. Peter Sellers did a very amusing impersonation of such aspiring stars. Gordy had made Diana a star of radio, certainly, and of the stage in terms of Las Vegas and New York spectaculars. He'd also made her a star of the small screen. But the larger one remained unconquered.

Several plans to produce a film of the life of Billie Holiday, perhaps the greatest jazz singer ever, had been discussed but none had reached the shooting stage. Ross was tested and cast for Paramount's treatment of the story, to be based, very loosely, on part of Holiday's life, drawing some material and its title from her autobiography. The film is dealt with in detail in Chapter 9, which covers all three movies made by Ross in the seventies. Suffice it to say here that her work on the film, recording the soundtrack and, later, publicizing the film, took up virtually all of 1972 and made her own records run a poor third place to the film and to her family. On 30 October 1972 Diana had her second daughter, Tracee. That month the film was premièred in the United States. In Britain, Motown pulled together six of her American and British hits, added half a dozen of her most popular album tracks, and put the selection out as a *Greatest Hits* package.

By the end of 1972 the movie soundtrack was in the American stores and plans had been laid for her to visit Europe in the spring of 1973 for a tour and to attend the premières of the film in various cities throughout Europe, and generally publicize the movie's existence. Ultimately, it was decided to postpone the concerts until the autumn and concentrate her energies during the trip on promoting the film. Although none of the film's featured songs reached the top twenty as singles on either side of the Atlantic, her performance of 'Good Morning Heartache' sold quite well and just made the American rhythm and blues top twenty.

Jetting around to do the right things by the film had an adverse effect on the quality of her albums. The next studio set, *Touch Me in the Morning*, was the first in a disquieting series on which she worked with several producers under the executive production of Berry Gordy. Albums had become, as in the Supremes' days, low on the totem pole of endeavour.

On *Touch Me* there were no fewer than seven different producer credits on the ten songs, two of which she produced herself. This working pattern, which became a normal procedure at Motown in the seventies, was the new relation to the old habit in the sixties of artists on the road rushing into the studio, singing their vocals on to prepared tracks in as few takes as possible, and going straight back on the road again, hardly pausing for breath. To continue the practice in the seventies, when albums had become a much more important part of the industry, was foolhardy or courageous, depending on one's point of view, but it was certainly not the way to win new fans or, indeed, keep those recently won by the film role.

Touch Me was an album influenced by Diana's preoccupation with having babies. On the second side of the album 'Little Girl Blue', 'My Baby (My Baby, My Own)', 'Brown Baby', 'Save the Children' and John Lennon's 'Imagine' strung a thread of birth and infancy through the music, though it became perhaps rather too self-involved for mass appeal. Of the fact that she was working with so many producers on one project, Diana said that only by working with an established act could Motown see how good a new writer or producer or arranger was going to be. Commercial success was more likely, therefore the potential was easier to spot. This, she admitted, might be rather tough on her, but she added that she was happy enough to be used as 'a vehicle through which they can learn'. The title track, written by Michael Masser and Ron Miller and produced by Masser and Tom Baird, and 'All of My Life', a showy song written, arranged and produced by Michael Randall, became hits – the former a number one in the USA and nine in Britain, the latter a big hit only in Britain, again reaching ninth place.

In the time between those two singles Marvin Gaye, who had taken two years to record his follow-up studio album to *What's Goin' On* (a soundtrack LP, *Trouble Man*, had intervened), was just scoring with another smash album, the sensual *Let's Get It On*. The temptation to pit their most glamorous woman with one of their sexiest male singers was not the sort of thing to which Motown was likely to show much resistance once the idea was formed, especially since both Diana (with the Temptations) and Marvin Gaye (with Mary Wells, Kim Weston and Tammi Terrell) had proven adept, and highly profitable, duettists.

Their ten-track album *Diana and Marvin* used five producers, but as Hal Davis was responsible for six of the tracks a sense of solidity and continuity pervaded it. Such a combination of star names was certain to sell records. Gaye's high tenor with its urgent, pleading tone and, on softer songs, an elegant, caressing grace, complemented Ross's less rangy vocals. At the end of 1973 one track, 'You're a Special Part of Me', produced by Berry Gordy, had gone into the American top twenty.

By then Diana had been to Europe on a triumphant tour during which she had played three nights in September at London's Royal Albert Hall plus concerts in Manchester, Liverpool, Glasgow and Newcastle. These were her first concerts in Britain since she'd left the Supremes and that fact, added to the admiration her film debut had won, ensured full houses and the glittering performances drew rave receptions and reviews. The excesses which came from playing to Las Vegas audiences, where flashiness for its own sake and the empty gesture are essential practice, had not yet swamped her performances. She was a believably glamorous star.

The songs in her shows were drawn from solo hits, a Supremes' medley, show tunes from *West Side Story* and *Jesus Christ Superstar*, Broadway showstoppers such as 'Don't Rain on My Parade', and newer American tunes such as 'Green' from the *Sesame Street* TV series. (It was the song associated with one of the puppet series' star characters, Kermit the Frog, 'compère' of *The Muppet Show*.)

From playing the role of a great jazz singer to singing a composition made famous by a frog, Diana had negotiated the first three years of solo work with great commercial success and no small amount of artistic acclaim. Her screen performance had been nominated for an Oscar for Best Actress (it went that year to Liza Minnelli for her role as Sally Bowles in *Cabaret*) and she had won many other awards and trophies – a Golden Globe for Best New Star, for instance, and *Cue Magazine*'s Entertainer of the Year title. And she had found time to marry, set up home in Beverly Hills and have two daughters.

69

6. DO YOU KNOW WHERE YOU'RE GOING TO?

In December 1973 Diana Ross released another studio album, *The Last Time I Saw Him*. Again it was a patchwork set, a motley collection of tracks using four producers on the ten songs. The title track was an American top twenty hit in February 1974, but it really was the most unappealing piece of jolly-sounding nonsense and typified the lackadaisical approach that was becoming rather too habitual on her solo albums.

In Britain, the 1974 singles release schedule was remarkable for the number of tracks lifted from the *Diana and Marvin* duet album. 'You're a Special Part of Me' began the chain in 1973 and was followed in 1974 by 'You Are Everything' (March), 'Stop, Look, Listen (to Your Heart)' (June) and 'My Mistake (Was to Love You)' (October; it had been an American single back in January). 'Don't Knock My Love' was a small hit in the USA in July. By contrast the releases from her studio album of that year were sparing: the title track on both sides of the Atlantic, plus 'Sleepin' ' in the United States in April and 'Love Me' in Britain in September. The comparatively poor sales of her singles suggested that while her audience would still flock to see her, it would no longer tolerate second-rate album tracks, and the floating buyer, whose custom would normally put her singles into the charts, was singularly unimpressed. If she wished to be seen as a bona fide album artist, she would have to spend time on an album, and choose songs worthy of such a reputation.

While other Motown artists such as Stevie Wonder, Marvin Gaye and the Jackson Five had shown an awareness of what was happening in other areas of black and white pop and rock in the United States, Diana's recordings had hardly progressed in the last couple of years. They were biased towards middle-of-the-road ballads, the cabaret crowd, and took no account of yet more changes in black American music.

In Philadelphia, at the Sigma Sound Studios, producers Kenny Gamble and Leon Huff's Philadelphia International set-up had developed a classy, powerful, orchestral sound centred on the MFSB band. With such artists as the O'Jays and Harold Melvin and the Blue Notes featuring Teddy Pendergrass they had very quickly built up an enormous reputation as *the* hot team and were attracting writers, musicians, arrangers and singers as Motown had done over a decade before in Detroit. And their material blended social comment-type songs with love songs in an attractive and consistent format.

Moreover, it seemed that a mass market was rediscovering dance music. To a certain extent, of course, the market had never disappeared, though for a couple of years actually to admit to enjoying modern black American music, and to like dancing, did elicit looks of profound pity in both Europe and the United States. There had always been a strong underground following for black dance music and it was always likely to produce a dozen or so smash hits a year. But with the impetus of the Philly Sound, other areas away from the centres of New York and Los Angeles suddenly started throwing up acts whose sound seemed indigenous to its area, even to a single studio. What they all had in common was a new, lively dance beat.

The Miami Sound was rooted in a small set of labels under the TK banner, and when George McCrae's 'Rock Your Baby' went to number one on both sides of the Atlantic in the summer of 1974 the event was generally regarded as the arrival of a new boom in discotheques and dancing. That group of labels went on to establish KC and the Sunshine Band, who were led by Howie Casey and Rick Finch, also the label's best pop writers and producers, as a top disco group. Similarly, in New Jersey, the All Platinum label had a sudden flush of success but couldn't sustain the early hits of the Moments and Shirley and Co.

The explosion of self-contained black bands still resounded and Motown finally responded to this change in audience taste by signing the Commodores from Tuskegee, Alabama. But the label's relationship with the group and producer James Carmichael was more like that which had prevailed with Stevie Wonder since 1971 – the finished album was delivered and Motown just manufactured and distributed it. The group has handsomely repaid the label for this freedom and has become one of the top three black bands in the United States.

Of the elder Motown artists, only Stevie Wonder was continually scoring high on the pop and rhythm and blues charts. Even the Jackson Five's popularity was waning as relations began to sour between the label and their father and business manager Joe Jackson. Eventually, they left the label for Epic.

Of greater importance to Diana's recording career was the fact that the gap she had left in the market by taking a year off to film and promote *Lady Sings the Blues*, with little more than filler tracks left behind to cover her absence, had quickly been filled. Aretha Franklin, ever softening her work, had six rhythm and blues hits in 1972–3 including three number ones; Roberta Flack had five hits; Gladys Knight and the Pips had seven, including three number ones. Aretha's performances of 'Angel' and 'Until You Come Back to Me (That's What I'm Gonna Do)', Flack's of 'First Time Ever I Saw Your Face', 'Killing Me Softly with His Song' and, with Donny Hathaway, 'Where Is the Love', and Knight's of 'Help Me Make It through the Night', 'Neither One of Us (Wants to Be the First to Say Goodbye)' and 'Midnight Train to Georgia' were all cross-over ballads which appealed to the MOR cabaret market, which Ross had once claimed for her own, *and* to the pop and rhythm and blues markets. The fact that the hits were delivered

with tenderness or emphatic emotion, depending on the requirement of the lyric, made Diana's apparent lack of commitment to her recent material, which admittedly invited little such commitment, seem all the more obvious, and the performances all the more hackneyed and hollow.

Even the Supremes' position as the top female vocal trio had been torn from their grasp by Philly's Three Degrees and Barry White's similarly lush, danceable confections with Love Unlimited.

In 1974 there was no respite from this trend. Flack had another number one record with 'Feel Like Makin' Love'; Knight had four rhythm and blues hits, two number ones and two cross-overs to the pop charts; Franklin had three rhythm and blues hits, one number one which also crossed into the pop top twenty. Against this Diana could claim three rhythm and blues hits, two of which were duets. The highest position she reached was fifteen. She had two pop top twenty hits on each side of the Atlantic, two of which were duets. Her only other album of the year was a live set recorded in Las Vegas and titled variously *Live! At Caesar's Palace* (USA) and simply *Live!* (UK).

On 5 November 1974 Diana had her third daughter, Chudney, and later that month work started on her second movie, *Mahogany*. Again, the film will be dealt with in Chapter 9. The film took up a large portion of 1975. While she was thus out of commission, her recorded output came almost to a standstill and, as she later admitted, her career during 1974–6 had no real plan behind it.

In February 1975 'Sorry Doesn't Always Make It Right', a single, was released world-wide. It was a Michael Masser/Pam Sawyer ballad, produced by Masser, who had previously done 'Touch Me in the Morning' and 'Last Time I Saw Him' and seemed at home with this torchy material. In Britain, another duet track with Gaye, 'Don't Knock My Love', was released to tide over the fallow spell.

Finally, in the autumn of 1975, the theme song from *Mahogany*, 'Do You Know Where You're Going to', written by Masser and Gerry Goffin and produced by Masser, was released along with the film and the soundtrack album. The single did considerably better than the film, which met with generally poor reviews,

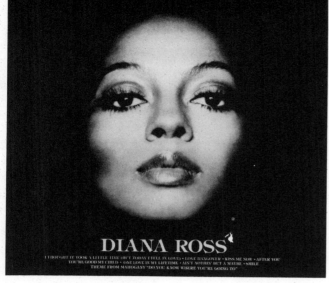

mostly lamenting that such a flimsy vehicle should have been chosen to follow her fine debut in *Lady*. Nevertheless, the theme tune had put her back in the charts.

That single reappeared on her next studio album, *Diana Ross*, out in Britain in the early months of 1976, in time for a tour scheduled to coincide with the British première of *Mahogany*. Yet another conglomeration of tracks from various production sources, *Diana Ross* still managed to give the impression that rather more care had been expended on the choice of songs and their arrangements. In addition to the *Mahogany* theme, Masser did two other tracks, one of which, 'I Thought It Took a Little Time (but Today I Fell in Love)' had a notable Gene Page arrangement which moderated Masser's tendency towards overwrought production.

But the album's highlight, indeed the best track she had recorded for some years, was produced by Hal Davis, who had done tracks with her towards the end of the Supremes' period and in the early seventies. The song, written by Pam Sawyer and Marilyn McLeod and given an excellent two-part arrangement by Dave Blumberg, was 'Love Hangover'.

The now fast-expanding disco market had produced a demand for longer tracks. As DJs had learned to segue one track into another, dancers had come to expect to be on the dance floor for, at the very least, ten to fifteen minutes without hearing a break in tempo. Thus the accepted length of the radio-orientated single, which was three minutes, became obsolete as far as disco DJs were concerned. Those black artists who had been influenced by rock had also developed a willingness to stretch out, and James Brown had for years been letting his funk tracks run on over five and six minutes. Marvin Gaye, too, on his *What's Goin' On* and *Let's Get It On* albums, had attempted to blend tracks into each other so that each side created a uniform mood of its own, if not precisely a uniform tempo. Several European producers were among the quickest to seize on this demand for long dance tracks. With their cold, hard, robotic-sounding backings, Giorgio Moroder and Pete Bellotte from Munich were turning Donna Summer into the number one black vocalist, in terms of record sales, in the world.

'Love Hangover' was Diana Ross's answer to this trend and it was conclusive. She eschewed the normal disco ploy of setting the tempo from bar one and letting the bass drum do all the work. Instead, after a shivery cascade of strings, the arrangement called for the first three minutes of the song to be taken at a swaying, after-glow pace – all sighs and cooing vocals – until, about halfway through the cut, a final, trilling sigh and sustained vocal note gives way to a pulsating dance rhythm led by hi-hat 'shushing' beside a hypnotic lead guitar figure which weaves around the bass guitar riff while an electric piano vamps enthusiastically in the background. The rhythm is occasionally boosted by handclaps on the off-beat before the vocals of Ross and her background singers return to play around with the melody, whispering and giggling, gently growling. The strings rejoin the mix, the drummer suddenly rediscovers his bass drum and the track fades, doubtless leaving the band to continue the fun for another ten minutes in the studio. It has that sort of endless groove.

Amazingly enough, Motown didn't issue this track as the first single off *Diana Ross*. 'I Thought It Took a Little Time', one of the Masser make-weights, was released in February 1976 in the United States. The Fifth Dimension announced that their version of 'Hangover', on ABC, would be released at once and Motown was sent into a flurry of activity. Ross's single of the song was out within the month and became her biggest hit for several years.

In Britain, the April release of the single was hard on the heels of Diana's second British tour. It was a longer tour than the first, and she played concerts in Birmingham, Bournemouth and Leicester, three at London's New Victoria Theatre, Southport, Glasgow, Edinburgh, Blackpool and Manchester. It was part of a long European tour which would touch down in Holland, Belgium, France, Germany, Italy and Switzerland.

The show was even more lavish than her last. Costing £250,000 to stage and lasting ninety minutes, it featured a thirty-eight-piece orchestra with her own special eight-piece rhythm section, five background singers, plus five dancers/mime artists who worked on the choreography and staging of Joe

. . . her lavish live shows were by now so minutely staged and choreographed through costume changes that critics lamented the lack of genuine emotion. Here, she's caught during her act at the Palais des Congres, Paris, on 5 April

Layton, with whom Diana had worked since the beginning of the seventies. It was exotic stuff, showbizzy razzamatazz of the richest variety.

The performances included excerpts from Harry Nilsson's *The Point*, which often verged on the excruciatingly schmaltzy. It had a cabaret base built around standards like 'The Lady Is a Tramp', 'Smile', and 'Send In the Clowns'. Her previous 'rousing' opening number, 'Don't Rain on My Parade', was replaced by 'Here I Am', a similarly rather self-congratulating barnstormer. Mixed in were a few of her hits such as 'Touch Me in the Morning' and 'Love Hangover' which, in fact, she sang only briefly, spending most of the tune dancing to her own prerecorded vocals. She did impersonations of and tributes to Billie Holiday, Ethel Waters, Bessie Smith and Josephine Baker, a medley of Supremes' songs, a medley of Motown hits, songs from *A Chorus Line* and other solo hits, like 'Reach Out and Touch', in which the audience would be persuaded to grasp their neighbour's hand in brotherly friendship. That she actually managed to coax the majority of her audience of normally self-conscious Londoners, for example, to do so was no minor feat. Perhaps holding hands assuages mutual embarrassment. No matter what, the feeling remained that, although much happened in the show in physical terms, it was a shallow experience which relied on artificial devices rather than genuine emotional commitment from the artist. What the shows did confirm was that Diana had by now developed that intangible quality, charisma, which enabled her to use hollow showbiz conventions to her own ends.

After touring Britain and Europe, the show was taken back to the United States where she made her Broadway debut with it at the Palace Theatre. The first two weeks soon sold out, breaking the venue's box-office gross by taking $427,901.50. The show was held over for an extra week. When she reached the Ahmanson Theatre in Los Angeles, the concert was recorded for a live double album, *An Evening with Diana Ross*, which came out at the very start of 1977, following a second *Greatest Hits* package in Britain in July 1976 (which was her first in the States).

Continued on page 91.

Far left: Under the unforgiving eye of the television camera Diana's beauty and glamour are undiminished

Left: Rhonda Suzanne makes her point. Diana's elder daughter looks on as Mom sings songs from Harry Nilsson's The Point

Below: Diana – the glamorous star, the beautiful woman

Far left: Diana! Live! A performer full of vitality and passion
Left & below: The lady sings the blues

Right: Diana, her orchestra and fans at London's Royal Albert Hall

Middle right: Someday we'll be together – the final encore

Far right: Reach Out and Touch Somebody's Hand

Below: Diana offers her mike to one of her brass section during a muted trumpet solo

Diana Ross is Billie Holiday. From the film The Lady Sings the Blues *in which Diana portrays the acclaimed jazz singer and tragic drug addict, driven to attacking her lover to get her fix*

Right: Diana cracks a joke between songs

Below: Ain't no mountain high enough, which is plain to see as yet another show works towards its stunning climax

But although 1976 had been a satisfying one for Diana through her return to the pop charts ('Love Hangover'), to the movie screen (*Mahogany*) and to lucrative touring, it had also been a year fraught with personal problems and tragedy. First, just as Diana's British dates were announced, the news broke of the death at the age of thirty-three of Florence Ballard. This sad event, of course, sent reporters hotfoot to Diana's press conference with an excellent angle on the story – one ex-Supreme announcing a quarter-of-a-million-pound show while another dies in Detroit after a cardiac arrest.

Florence had been living on welfare payments for a few years before her death. She had recently been reconciled with her husband and the couple, with their three daughters, had moved into a new home. Florence's solo career had come to nothing and in 1971 she had filed a $3 million damages suit against Motown. Diana's answer to the questions about Ballard's death was that Florence had made her own decisions and had refused help when it was offered, preferring to make it alone if she could. Whatever the details, Diana set up a trust fund for Florence's children and Motown matched the offer, which in the circumstances it could hardly fail to do. But perhaps the most fulsome tribute to Florence came from Mary Wilson, still keeping the Supremes going but by now thinking about a solo career of her own. She told *Blues and Soul* magazine: 'Florence gave more to the Supremes than the group gave to her. It was her name and it was her perseverance that kept us going during the hard days. People loved Florence for what she was. Though she stayed in the background, it was her strong presence that we all fell back on for our support. When she left, I began to realize that it was no longer a game and I saw just how cruel the world could be.

'I guess the main problem was that Florence grew disillusioned with Motown as they pulled Diana into the foreground . . . it was upsetting and we simply never came to an understanding once Diana had her name out front.'

Florence's death was the latest, and infinitely the most tragic, in the long series of rumours and hints of scandal which had surrounded the close-knit Motown operation virtually from the day Gordy

That parting of the ways between Diana and her husband came in 1977. Cause: 'irrenconcilable differences'. The picture far right captures the mood of 1976-7. Very, very mixed

started business. To outsiders the label seemed secretive, and its phenomenal success from the very beginning suggested Mephistopholean forces at work. Gossip was fuelled by the very public tragedies – such as Tammi Terrell's collapse on stage and her subsequent death after operations for a brain tumour – and the disgruntled complaints of the stream of acts enticed from the label towards the end of the sixties and at the start of the seventies by the promise of full attention and big money from other labels. For years there had been murkier stories of heavy involvement in Motown by organized crime syndicates. Between the public fact, the artists' gripe and the Mafioso murmur is a large, grey fog into which only the intrepid may venture with confidence. These 'stories' are endlessly intriguing to white pop journalists, whose view of Motown and its top stars has become more and more jaundiced through the last decade, and who prefer the glib generalization (Motown is too big, too Los Angeles-laid back and therefore bad) to the particularization.

What need had the label to get into cahoots with the Mafia? One theory has it that very early on Gordy's company may have got into financial difficulties when money earned by the first big hit, 'Shop Around', was slow to come in from record stores via the distributors, and that large loans to pay bills and finance other recording and promotions were needed. The Mafia's greatest need, it has been suggested, to move into a thriving new industry like recording came around 1964, when it had suffered severe gambling losses in the Caribbean and Central America.

The temptation to factionalize such gossip into novel form proved too great for one ex-Motown employee, Elaine Jesmer. Her *Number One with a Bullet* purported to be a thinly veiled account of the career of Marvin Gaye. It was a work of literature that did her subject scant justice. Motown employees tend to smile ruefully and clam up when these matters are mentioned – frequently because they themselves know only rumours, not facts, and they are mentioned here merely in order to give some idea of the gossip-mongering atmosphere in which Diana's, and most original Motown artists' careers had long existed.

Pretty soon gossip columnists were given fresh meat for their slabs. Although the marriage with Robert Silberstein had produced three daughters and was, outwardly, happy enough, the demands of Diana's touring, recording and filming, and Silberstein's own busy career, meant that they were often apart for long periods. So when the couple split up for a trial period of about five months, no one took undue notice. But there were other pressures besides those exerted by business. Diana was black and Christian; Silberstein was white and Jewish. Even in the supposedly enlightened seventies, the mixed marriage of race and religion, if not openly frowned upon, still caused the more 'sensitive' some dismay. Without the weight of two showbusiness careers, this would have been difficult enough to support. With it, the marriage finally buckled. Diana filed for divorce on the grounds of 'irreconcilable differences' at the Los Angeles Superior court in 1977. However, soon afterwards Silberstein made this illuminating comment: 'My wife belongs to that company. She's totally dominated by a man who never read a book in his life.' Mr Silberstein's experience as a public relations executive dealing with the media certainly left him with a sharp ear for the quotable. It was also noted that even when the Silbersteins had been able to have a rare family holiday and go off into the mountains, it was not unknown for Gordy to join the party.

Diana's 1976 had been a very mixed year.

7. THE BOSS

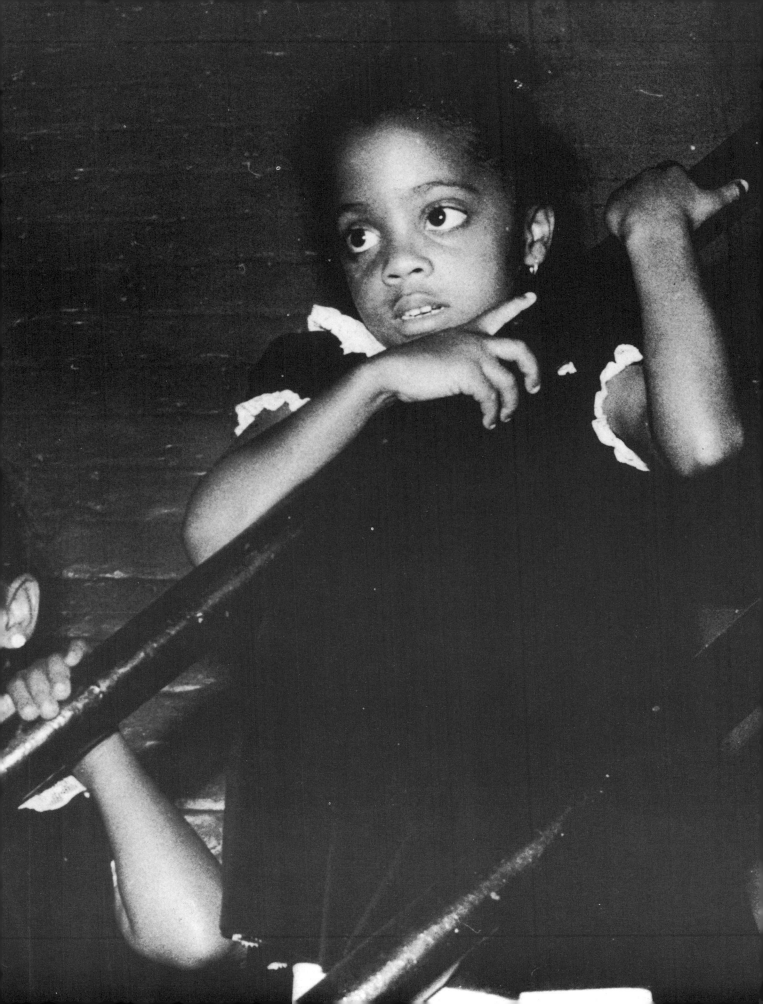

Diana Ross's career during 1974–6 had been characterized by its haphazard nature. When all around her were allying themselves to the disco or funk markets, she seemed content to drift aimlessly in the MOR stream. The next years would see a new definition given to her recording career.

But first, in the summer of 1976, Motown acquired the film rights to the musical *The Wiz*, an all-black adaptation of *The Wizard of Oz* which had been running successfully on Broadway. The starring role of Dorothy – the character played by Judy Garland in the original movie – became one of the most sought-after for years and it was a surprise when Diana won it in the face of competition from other black singer/actresses who had played the role on stage. Since *Lady Sings the Blues* Diana had become a bankable box office movie star. That, combined with her close ties to Motown and her powers of persuasion, got her the part. Once again, the making and merit of the film are discussed in Chapter 9, but winning the role was to affect Diana's lifestyle enormously.

The Wiz was to be set and filmed entirely in New York. Coming hard on the heels of her divorce petition, the role and its location gave her the excuse to move east. If she were to have a break with her Los Angeles lifestyle, let it be as complete as possible. The film was a long time in the making and would not be premièred until late 1978. In the meantime, Diana turned to her by now inconsistent, flagging recording career. At last she was placed with one producer for a whole album.

Richard Perry had made his name as a producer of luxurious-sounding adult-orientated rock albums by singers such as Leo Sayer and Carly Simon. He had attempted, unsuccessfully, to engineer the comeback on record of Martha Reeves. Perry's forte was the selection of songs, often from unexpected or long-forgotten sources, and reworking them in an easy-listening, soft-rock format. His work with Reeves hadn't been particularly outstanding – her voice seemed uncomfortably restrained in the too-perfect surroundings. On Diana's *Baby It's Me* album Perry struck a more satisfactory balance. Of course Diana's voice, less assertive, rough and edgy than Reeves', was far more suited to the songs and the settings provided by Perry, his arrangers – who included

Gene Page, Del Newman and David Foster – and a team of his usual seasoned, but young, LA session musicians.

When *Baby It's Me* was released, in October 1977, its mixture of light rock, with slight bows in the direction of disco and ballads, was again somewhat at odds with the general bias of commercial music. The greater certainty with which Moroder and Bellotte were producing Donna Summer and the mindless, occasionally witty effusions of the Village People made the Ross/Perry collaboration sound slightly dry. The album, however, has lasted better than her other mid-seventies' albums simply because it has that wholeness which comes from a single producer's vision of what an artist should be.

Two old Jerry Ragovoy co-compositions – 'All Night Lover' (with Len Roberts) and 'You Got It' (with Linda Laurie) – harked back to the melodies of the sixties, and the arrangements combined a sixties' base with the calmer, more controlled delivery of the seventies. 'Your Love Is So Good to Me' gave a fine example of Perry's gentle genuflections towards disco, while the confident, swingy 'Gettin' Ready for Love', Stevie Wonder's lush ballad 'Too Shy to Say', and the torchier 'Confide in Me' gave some idea of the wide range of styles Perry pulled together within the narrow emotional range of middle-of-the-road rock.

Diana's commitment to filming *The Wiz* and recording its soundtrack precluded the recording of much new material for some time, so it was fortuitous that the album with Perry was so broad-based in appeal. Three singles were lifted from it between October 1977 and June 1978: 'Gettin' Ready for Love'; 'Your Love Is So Good to Me' (in the USA) and 'Top of the World' (in the UK); then 'Your Love' in Britain and 'You Got It' in the United States. Diana sold up her twelve-room Beverly Hills mansion and moved her three children and yellow Rolls Royce to Manhattan, where the family settled into the Sherry Netherland building.

There was little time in 1977 for extensive touring – though Diana did play a one-off concert at the Forest Hills lawn tennis stadium in July – but by 1978 she was back on the road. She was to be one of the main attractions in an ultimately abortive plan by

. . . how much nine hours in the make-up department can ruin a girl's looks. For her March 1977 NBC TV Special, An Evening With Diana Ross, *the star underwent what looks like major cosmetic surgery to portray (left to right) Ethel Waters, Josephine Baker and Bessie Smith*

Townsend Thoresen, the travel firm, to celebrate their fiftieth anniversary with a series of concerts at the London Palladium. Also featured would be stars such as Perry Como, Petula Clark, the Carpenters, Barry White and Helen Reddy. Thoresen pulled out of the project but several of the concerts were salvaged, and Diana played at the theatre on 4, 5 and 6 May, doing two shows each night.

By now prices for the most expensive seats had soared to £20. The set was as Las Vegas-showbiz as ever. The performance was based on the same songs she had brought to London two years previously. Some of the effects, if not exactly stunning, were still fairly spectacular. At the very start of the show the long train of her gown was unfurled by two mimes, and shots from the film *Mahogany* were projected on to this improvized screen. Other parts of the show, such as the moment she held an impromptu press conference with the audience, inviting questions, were more like the aberrations of a star who had spent too long performing for cabaret and supper club audiences and couldn't adapt to an audience from a different country with different expectations.

The concerts sold out but so, the critics unanimously pronounced, had Diana Ross. This was not much more than they had been saying for the previous two or three years, at the very least. She had become the sort of artist whose audience is reviewed for its opulence. The basic staginess of her presentations and her enforced 'closeness' to her fans only reinforced the distance between the two. She was among the people, but plainly unapproachable, up there in the stratosphere. The same contrast between the singles artist and the album artist/live entertainer remained, and seemed to be magnified a good many times by the shows.

By September 1978 she was back on the West Coast playing the Los Angeles Universal Amphitheatre, and her set had altered sufficiently to include seven new songs from *The Wiz* and even more extravagant stagings, climaxing with the moment when Diana was carried on stage in an enormous pink shoe to sing 'To Love'. That song was from her new album, *Ross*. After the Perry experiment, it was a considerable disappointment to find her back on the discordant Motown production style of using several producers

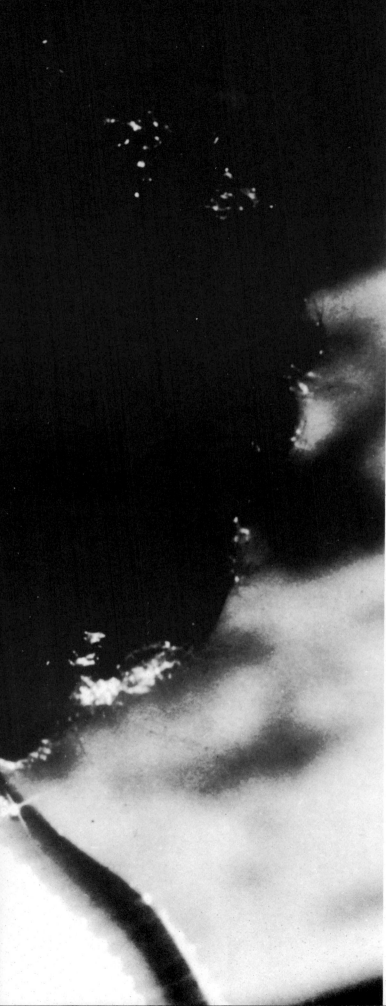

on one album. On the bright side, she was reunited with Hal Davis who had consistently proved a sympathetic collaborator on her solo tracks, and on 'Lovin', Livin' and Givin' ' and 'What You Gave Me' he and arranger Art Wright provided solid disco tracks. The latter was a Nick Ashford and Valerie Simpson song and consequently had more melody than the single-minded electronic disco feel of 'Lovin' ', which was used on the soundtrack of the Donna Summer movie *Thank God It's Friday*. But those tunes apart, *Ross* was another failure. Of its nine tracks, only six were new recordings. Two old Michael Masser productions ('Together' and 'Sorry Doesn't Always Make It Right') and one 1971 Ashford and Simpson production ('Reach Out, I'll Be There') were dusted off to flesh out the album. While all this was perhaps understandable in the light of her filming and touring work, it still seemed poor value and made a rather shoddy package from a singer now widely regarded as a leading *femme fatale* superstar. The two Hal Davis tracks were lifted as singles off the album, although only 'What You Gave Me' was issued in the United States.

Diana joined the rest of the Motown roster on an album titled *Pops We Love You*, through which the label's stars paid tribute to Berry Gordy Sr, who had reached the grand old age of ninety in 1978. That he died soon after the release of the title track as a single should not be taken as drastic, irrevocable comment on the song. If nothing else, the single was collectable since it featured Diana, Stevie Wonder, Marvin Gaye and Smokey Robinson together on one song.

The failure of *Ross*, and of her third movie, prompted positive action from Motown to revitalize her recording career. By now she had fallen decisively under the shadow of Donna Summer and other new artists spawned by the disco boom of the mid-seventies. One of the teams with whom she had recorded many fine sides, Ashford and Simpson, had become one of the hottest writing and production teams as well as being hit-makers and performers in their own right.

From the start of their writing partnership, Ashford and Simpson had used the more positive lyrical notions and expressions which were increasingly the concern of black Americans. But this positive lyrical

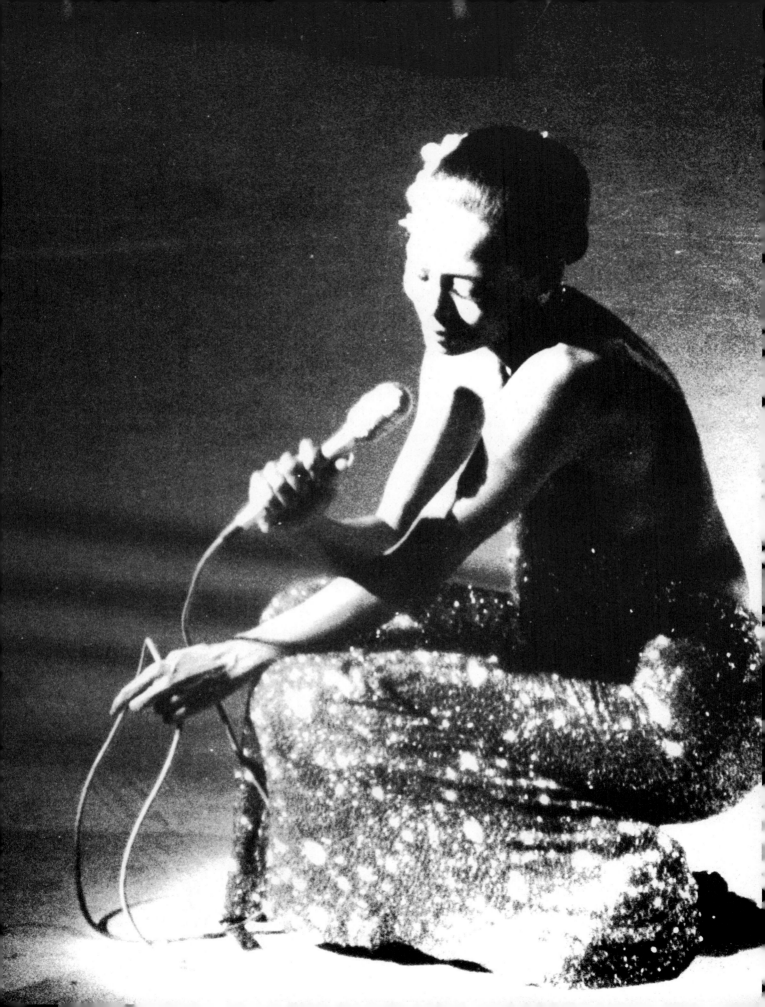

Diana and actress Ingrid Bergman (far right) are honoured with special Cesar awards in France – Diana's was for her work in Lady Sings The Blues. *Her stage shows (near right) remained stagey extravaganzas but her album performances improved significantly with the Nickolas Ashford and Valerie Simpson-produced* The Boss *(below right)*

outlook hadn't weakened the power of the gospel-derived melodies and arrangements. Past history and current form suggested that a rematch between Ross and Ashford and Simpson ought to result in fireworks. Moreover, the duo was based on the East Coast, and now that Diana had moved to Manhattan the teaming became even more sensible. When Ashford and Simpson worked now, they did so with total control, and since Diana had been cutting her closest ties with Berry Gordy, working with them would be another expression of freedom. The album, *The Boss*, was in fact the first since she went solo on which Gordy was not credited as producer or executive producer. Even its title did more than hint at self-assurance.

Her producers wrote eight new songs for the album and did the rhythm tracks with a team of East Coast session musicians with whom they usually worked at that time. Ashford and Simpson drew a far more interesting succession of performances from Diana than had been heard on a whole album for some years. Perry's *Baby It's Me* had been fitful, but on *The Boss* she began to find reliable, commanding form. The growing confidence of her singing throughout a track called 'All for One', the sureness and defiance expressed in 'I Ain't Been Licked' and the growing conviction of her singing on the title track (on which she sounds as though she is following the producers' demo vocal exclamation for exclamation) all confirmed the impression of returning enthusiasm for recording now that the project was being treated with sense and understanding.

The title track, 'No One Gets the Prize' and 'It's My House' were all hit singles in Britain. Only the first- and last-named tracks were released on forty-five in the USA. 'House' is an especially beguiling little song and so untypical of both the writers and performer. Diana sings confidently against an uncomplicated background of simple rhythm section working unfussily on a smooth, light mid-tempo, a deft horn arrangement by John Davis, some dainty flute and percussion colouring and Eric Gale picking a gentle electric guitar figure. Although utter charm was not a valued quality in the contemporary music scene, this track had so much of it and rejoiced so unaffectedly in the fact that it was impossible to resist. *The Boss* was released in the United States in May and a month later in Britain. Diana went on a six-week, thirty-city American tour to promote the LP. Her orchestra had swollen to fifty pieces and she worked with nine dancers and thirteen singers.

Later in 1979, Motown in Britain put together a *20 Golden Greats* compilation album for UK release only, as part of the EMI policy of putting out such packages for heavy promotion through TV advertising. Released in time for the Christmas market, just five months after *The Boss* and on top of three hit singles, there was little reason to doubt the commercial wisdom behind its release.

So, after a few years during which Diana had reassessed her life completely, she was at last emerging as a stronger performer and woman. She had her children and a new home in Manhattan, and was beginning to assume fuller control over her life and work. She had every reason to look forward to the eighties with confidence.

8. COMING OUT

← Trans

← Transfers

1980: A blockbuster year for Diana and she was looking in perfect condition for it, both in the shot for the inside of her hit album, Diana, or (near left) catching a New York-bound flight in February after taping a Muppet Show

By 1979 Bernard Edwards and Nile Rodgers were one of the hottest writing and producing teams in pop music after just a couple of years. Like Ashford and Simpson, they were also excellent musicians and hit recording artists leading the group Chic, which they had formed. Via that group, Edwards and Rodgers had developed an instantly recognizable style of disco based on Edwards' strong, supple bass guitar lines, Rodgers' energetic rhythm guitar chording and pungent riff picking, and the solid, simple drumming of Tony Thompson. Their songs had tremendously catchy hooks and lyrics of suavity, humour and unusual invention. Their basic rhythm tracks were coloured by clever use of keyboards and strings. Neither Edwards nor Rodgers had particularly good voices; when they devised the group, they felt that women's voices would sound better within its framework and Norma Jean Wright, Alfa Anderson and Luci Martin sang lead on Chic's records.

The group's unique sound came to dominate the disco scene for much of the1976–8 period, and the services of Edwards and Rodgers as writers and producers for others became much in demand. Norma Jean went solo and they produced her tracks; they made hits with Sister Sledge ('He's the Greatest Dancer' was an especially memorable disco single) and also recorded with star Sheila & B. Devotion, for whom they produced the hit 'Spacer' and a poor album. The release of that album coincided with the release of the group's own *Real People* LP and it appeared probable that the group had been spreading its ideas far too thinly. Their sound was no longer fresh, copyists abounded, their own writing had become predictable and their playing mannered. But the duo's work with women singers had proved sympathetic. They favoured a vocal delivery pitched somewhere between the light, breathy tone of Diana Ross and the more strident singing of Donna Summer.

By the end of 1979 it had been agreed that Edwards and Rodgers would write and produce Diana's next solo album. The way Chic worked suited her too: they laid down all the basic tracks and she would come in at a late stage in production to add her vocals. Diana had worked this way since she started going out on the road with the Supremes. Like Ashford and Simpson, the Chic organization recorded

109

Although Diana was on a private visit to London in the autumn of 1980 she stopped by (right) to pick up a few of the gold and platinum records which had accumulated during the year – for the single 'Upside Down' and the LPs Diana *(below left) and* 20 Golden Greats

in New York, which again suited Ross very well. However, when the final tapes for the album, to be called *Diana*, were delivered to Motown both she and her label expressed doubts about their quality and, with Russ Terrana, she substantially remixed them, bringing forward her vocals along with Thompson's drumming at the expense of the rest of Chic's accompaniments.

Edwards and Rodgers, who were not used to such interference, expressed distaste for the remixes. This was, happily, not a view shared by record buyers, who quickly made the album, released in the summer of 1980, one of Diana's biggest-selling solo sets. Three singles from the album – 'Upside Down', 'My Old Piano' and 'I'm Coming Out' – were all hits before the end of 1980 in Britain. The carry-over sales from 1979 of the *20 Golden Greats* compilation plus the success of the new album and singles sparked off a sales boom in her records – by the end of 1980 she had sold one million records in Britain alone in the twelve-month period. In a contracting market and depressed economy, this was a remarkable achievement. It not only showed that Diana's loyal fans remained so, but that the children whose parents had grown up with her music were still ready to seize those Ross records reflective of her true talent for good pop singing. The fact that she did this with a sound that had, in the producers' hands, started to seem slightly passé added to the quality of her final and complete commercial recovery in 1980.

The recovery wasn't *just* commercial, however. Despite the reservations of Rodgers and Edwards about the remixing of *Diana*, the set remains, along with the Ashford and Simpson albums and Hal Davis tracks, easily her best solo work to date. *Diana* had eight Edwards/Rodgers songs performed with the clear, clenched tightness which marked Chic's early tracks. On top of this background of marvellous economy and hard-gloss brightness, Diana's vocals glide and swank and croon breathily with a real sense of enjoyment.

When an artist works with producers or a group who have a distinctive sound there is a danger that he or she will become little more than a featured guest. There are moments when this seems likely on *Diana*, but generally her equally distinctive voice claims

Presented to
DIANA ROSS
to recognise sales in the United Kingdom
of more than 250,000 copies of the
MOTOWN single
"UPSIDE DOWN"
1980

What every single girl about town must look out for: once ubiquitous date Warren Beatty (top row, far left); rock star Alice Cooper (top row, centre); the clubs – near left is Club 78, Paris, whose owner, Patrice Calmettes, is showing off one of the disco's 'attractions'; working up a sweat (bottom left); and, in a more sedate moment, admiring the 1980 Yves St Laurent spring fashions with dancer Zizi Jeanmaire

most songs as hers to command. On ballads such as 'Friend to Friend' and on all three singles she is clearly the boss. Only, perhaps, on the up-tempo 'Tenderness', where the Chic voices of Alfa Anderson and Luci Martin, forcefully joined by regular Chic back-up singers Fonzi Thornton and Michelle Cobbs, does the tune seem dominated by choral rather than solo singing, and the sheer quantity of vocal dictates the final sound.

But there are some wonderful passages on the album. The fractured instrumental introduction to 'I'm Coming Out' was one of the most exciting on record that year, or any other year come to that. From Rodgers' furiously chording guitar to Thompson's blunderbuss bursts of snare, tom-tom and bass drum fire which mimic the chatty horn riffs, the pace and timing of the introduction is thrilling and surprising. While the out-of-the-closet lyric seemed both two years behind the times and rather coy, if one saw the words in terms of Diana's emergence from a sad and difficult period in her life, then her exuberant singing took on a far more personal character.

Her first hit of 1981 took the mood further. Another Michael Masser production/co-composition, 'It's My Turn', was the theme song of an eponymous movie firmly in the ballad tradition of past Ross/Masser collaborations which the singer could by now handle with consummate skill and ease. And indeed maybe it was her turn.

Since breaking up with Robert Silberstein she had become once again an object of some interest to gossip columnists. Simple dates became furtive romances. To be spotted in the company of Studio 54 boss Steve Rubell or the ubiquitous Warren Beatty, or film director Sidney Lumet when he was working on *The Wiz*, or Michael Jackson, or designer Danny Zarem, is to be sure that you will be in tomorrow's newspapers. Her most recent romance of any length was with Kiss guitarist Gene Simmons, a fairly left-field friendship. Kiss is a flashy heavy-metal band of minimal instrumental proficiency but vast appeal to young kids in the United States where Kiss comics and TV cartoons abound. The group goes in for garish stage make-up and costumes, blinding magnesium flashes and deafening volume.

It's the Muppet Show! Fozzie Bear looks in his element (near right) but (below) Miss Piggy doesn't seem to cherish being up-staged

Simmons' forte is quasi-lewd use of his waggling tongue, the alarming length of which is enhanced by gaudy facial decoration. He also spits blood on stage. He is a lot quieter off stage, except when photographers snap him without his make-up.

The romance was strong enough to entice Diana to Britain in 1980 when Kiss toured in December. She was also able then to catch label-mate Stevie Wonder at Wembley's Empire Pool and to sing there with Wonder and Marvin Gaye, who had been in London for a protracted visit. She had also visited Britain in February 1980 to tape a show with the Muppets. But these few appearances apart, she had concentrated on a quiet life and relaxation. While she has said she wants to remarry, she has also intimated that the romance with Simmons seems unlikely to go that far, though there is obviously a great deal of fondness in the relationship.

Producing other artists is something she's often talked about but never conclusively followed up with deeds. She did a couple of tracks with Devastating Affair, one of her vocal backing groups, and might have been expected to take a close interest in her sister Rita's recording career, which was getting under way in 1978. During her pregnancies, when not working on her own projects, she found employment in Motown's artist development department which looked for, signed and guided new talent on the label. But she has patently not been as active in the production and promotion of young talent as, say, Stevie Wonder.

House-hunting for a move out to the country in Connecticut occupied time, as have those sports which she most enjoys watching – baseball and boxing – and participating in – swimming and tennis. She loves gambling, doesn't smoke much and drinks little. It's obvious just by looking at her that she keeps herself in good condition physically.

But there could yet be more upheavals. Her recording contract with Motown expired at the end of 1980. Motown had at least one album's worth of material in the can and at the beginning of 1981 a compilation of Michael Masser productions, with three new tracks added, was released. The album was titled *To Love Again*, and as well as the recent 'It's My Turn' and the previous film theme of *Mahogany*, ('Do

You Know Where You're Going to'), the set included 'One More Chance', her early spring single.

Motown was renegotiating with her but she was also actively engaged in talking to other labels keen to sign her. As such, her appearances in February 1981 at the Inglewood Forum, her first Los Angeles show for two years, proved a timely shop window.

Finally, the end of an era. Diana left Motown in the late spring of 1981 and signed with RCA Records for Canada and North America and with Capitol Records for all other territories.

But whatever the label, Diana Ross's ageless pop singing will be with us for many, many years to come.

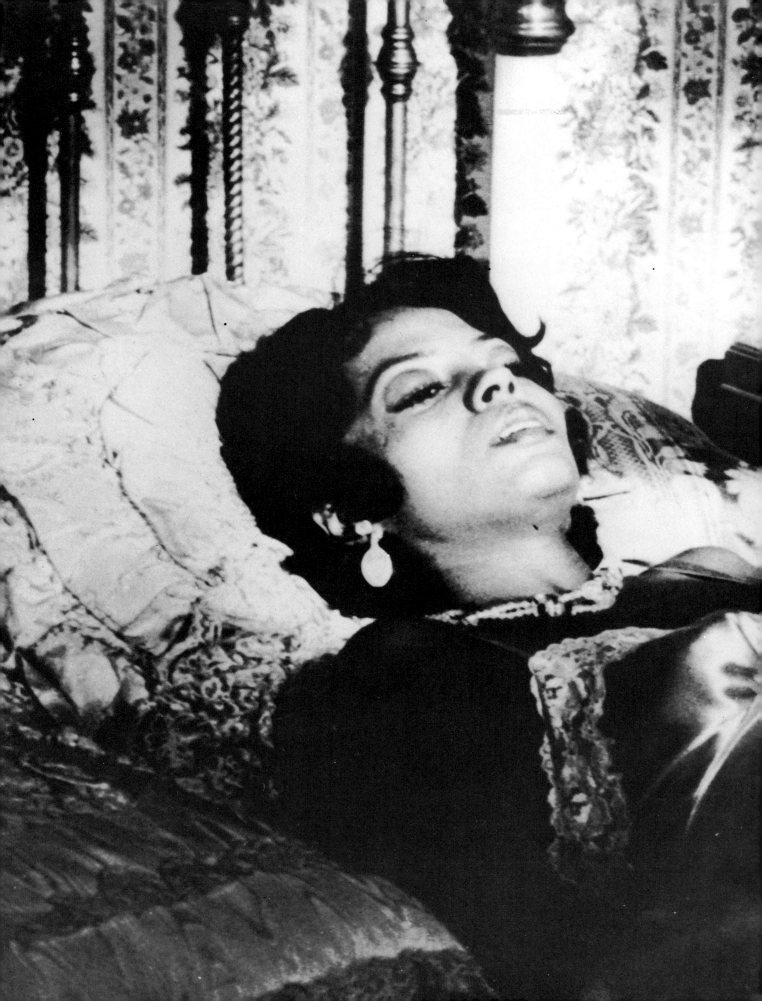

9. ROLL 'EM!

From the Paramount Picture Lady Sings the Blues, *Diana as the young Billie Holiday catching the ear and eye at an early club audition (far left and left)*

Black movies became fashionable in the American film business when Melvin Van Peebles' low-budget *Sweet Sweetback's Badasssss Song* became a cult hit among the ghetto population in the early seventies and earned the star, writer and director big bucks. Soon afterwards *Shaft* and *Superfly* followed, with bigger budgets from established studios, and their box-office success led to a spate of increasingly wretched 'blaxploitation' films which had little to recommend them other than an occasionally interesting soundtrack.

It had been part of Gordy's thinking that his move to California would smooth his company's entry into films when and if the opportunity arose. Diana Ross was his best-known star, and she was also photogenic. On her TV special, *Diana!*, and in other guest appearances on TV shows, she'd shown some aptitude, though within an admittedly narrow range, for impersonation and mild characterization.

By the end of 1971 negotiations, which had started in 1969 when Diana was still in the Supremes, were almost complete for her to play the role of Billie Holiday in the biopic *Lady Sings the Blues*. Motown had in the meantime turned down a starring role for her in *The Owl and the Pussycat* because she was to have played a whore. But the biopic could combine Gordy's celluloid ambitions with those of Ross. It would also be timely in view of the proliferation of movies starring black actors and actresses which were doing good business.

Although the film was based on Holiday's autobiography, *Lady Sings the Blues*, a considerable amount of licence was used in retelling the story of her life. The emotional and physical pain in her life were emphasized and occasionally made to seem glamorous in an 'art is suffering' way, while the periods of joy and great artistic achievement were rather too hurriedly passed over. The film would suggest that it was a white bandleader who first turned her on to the drugs which would ultimately kill her, but there is no real evidence as to the race of this man though it was thought to be one of her husbands. That scene, however, was validated in that it was used as a general illustration of the pressures put on black performers by white society – a fact even more vividly portrayed when Billie/Diana tours

the South with a predominantly white band and is refused service in a roadside café, witnesses a Ku Klux Klan meeting and march and eventually goes berserk yelling abuse at the parading racists while her travelling companions struggle to calm her and keep her from view and probable retribution.

Ultimately, despite the inaccuracies, the film worked admirably both as a portrayal of part of Billie's life and as a broad impression of a black artist's life in showbusiness in the forties and fifties. It was good film drama. More importantly, perhaps, the continuing struggle of a significant number of blacks with heroin and other drug problems made the film's social and anti-drug messages all the more potent.

The film was directed by Sidney Furie who had held out against opposition from the film's distributors to have Diana in the lead role. The screenplay was written by Terence McCloy, Chris Clark and Suzanne DePasse and music not taken from the Billie Holiday songbook was composed by Michel Legrand. Gil Askey, who later toured with Diana as her road orchestra's conductor, now conducted the orchestra on tunes associated with Holiday using his own, Benny Golson's and Oliver Nelson's arrangements.

Purists, almost inevitably, were outraged that anyone – let alone a pop singer who defined what they considered to be a grating, repetitive sound and style of dance music – should dare to impersonate Lady Day. But Ross's performance of some dozen-and-a-half songs which Holiday had popularized showed great respect for the originals while in no way attempting to make a voiceprint copy of every nuance of intonation. To prepare for the vocal work Diana listened to nothing but Billie Holiday records for something like six months. She looked at pictures of her and read the book over as well as any other cuttings she could find. She studied the speech and mannerisms of junkies and called on her own memories of pimps and prostitutes in Detroit. She gradually absorbed as much of the character as she was able. Holiday's was some story to take in.

When Billie's father and mother married at the ages of eighteen and sixteen, Billie was already three years old. She was sent to live with her aunt in Baltimore. Billie's naive mother thought the aunt

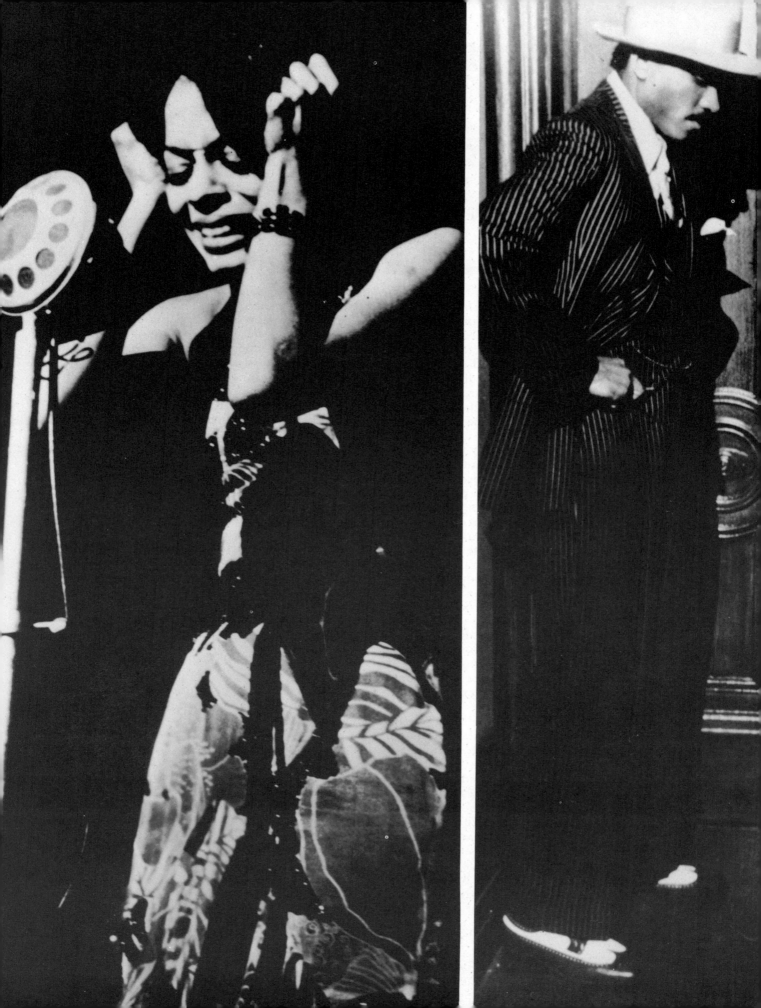

ran an hotel. In fact, auntie was a Madam. So Billie worked in the brothel, doing chores; eventually she was raped. (She was, in real life, raped at the age of ten.) She began singing in local clubs, was quickly spotted and went on to work with the bands of Artie Shaw, Count Basie and Benny Goodman and sang memorably with Lester Young and Teddy Wilson in small group settings which were probably her best performances. Indeed, it was the lack of recognition that such formative musicians as Wilson and Young received in the film's plot that upset many jazz buffs. Billie had four husbands and many lovers. In the film, they were distilled into one character, played by Billy Dee Williams, who struggled vainly to hold her life together. Yet it was likely that her first husband, whom she married in 1942, was a user and turned her on to drugs.

Just as her husbands/lovers were concentrated into one role, so the part of Piano Man, played by Richard Pryor, became the embodiment of all her musician friends who tried to help Billie by attempting to regulate her supply of drugs, keeping her amused and constantly involved in music. He is eventually killed while trying to get drugs to a badly strung-out Billie. Her arrests for drug possession, the inhuman incarcerations which followed, the powerful images of black oppression in the South (the song 'Strange Fruit' refers to, and is sung against, shots of the bodies of blacks, lynched by the Klan, hanging fruit-like from the branches of the trees) and of racial discrimination in general are all points tellingly made.

The film closes as Billie makes a triumphant appearance at Carnegie Hall. As she is cheered by an ecstatic, largely white, audience, newspaper headlines report the decline to follow through drug-associated arrests, the failure to obtain a licence to play cabaret in New York, and the final death scene when it took a court order to remove narcotics agents waiting by Billie's deathbed to arrest her in the unlikely event of her recovery. She was fifty-nine years old.

Whatever the varying opinions of the liberties taken with the precise story of Billie Holiday's life, the admiration for Diana Ross's performance in the role remains high. She held the attention in every scene – indeed she appeared in almost every scene, a

123

remarkably long time to be on camera – and certainly showed a strong grasp of what the film was trying to say through Holiday's life.

The film went into production on 6 December 1971, took forty-four days to shoot, and had the star in 168 scenes. For the first six days' shooting she played Billie as a teenager; by the eighth day she was in the Baltimore brothel; and by the fourteenth day she was playing Holiday on the road with the fictional Reg Hanley Band.

At one point in production, shortly after a scene in which Diana/Billie had been required to attack her 'husband' with a cut-throat razor in order to discover where he had hidden her stash of drugs, Billy Dee Williams was asked about Diana's acting skills. 'She *is* Billie Holiday' was his rueful reply after narrowly escaping severe lacerations. His reply caught the ear of the promotion department and, by the time *Lady Sings the Blues* was premièred at Loew's Theatre in New York on 17 October 1972, the posters, hoardings and press advertisements were proclaiming that 'Diana Ross IS Billie Holiday'. This piece of promotional hyperbole further infuriated the jazz purists. But the film was a runaway smash. The $3 million production grossed over $6 million in the first six weeks of release, and the soundtrack album sold 300,000 copies in America in the first eight days of release.

Reviews were full of praise for Diana's acting, while dutifully expressing reservations about the film's plot and the liberties taken with the exact truth of Billie's life. Even more enlightening were the views of the more elderly jazz critics and musicians – Max Jones and Beryl Bryden in Britain, and Ralph Gleason, John Hammond and Leonard Feather in the United States – who had known Billie and followed her closely. While accepting that her story was by no means intact, they felt that much of Diana's performance caught the spirit of the subject and that her singing was far from being an insult to the great jazz vocalist.

By the time the British version of the film, cut from the original 160 minutes in the USA to 125 minutes, was premièred in London on 4 April 1973, a whole Billie Holiday industry had grown up in the wake of the movie's success. One of the better side-

effects was the re-release in well-annotated packages of most of Billie's recordings. Several stage versions of her life were put into production and one jazz musical, *Lady Day*, starring Cecelia Norfleet at the Brooklyn Chelsea Theatre, was reviewed in less than complimentary terms.

When Diana was nominated for Best Actress at the Academy Awards of 1973 she was strongly tipped to win against another black actress, Cicely Tyson, in *Sounder*, as well as Maggie Smith and Liza Minnelli; Minnelli won for her portrayal of Sally Bowles in *Cabaret*. Though this was an obvious disappointment to Diana and Motown, *Lady Sings the Blues* had nevertheless established her as a reliable box-office draw able to command a hefty fee.

Lady Sings the Blues had been a Paramount film and they put Diana on a two-picture contract. Several projects were discussed. A remake of *A Couple of Swells* was mulled over but came to nothing, and later a film based on Richard Rodgers' *No Strings* stage musical, which had starred Diahann Carroll on Broadway, fell through, as did *Born Yesterday*. Finally a second Paramount project was agreed. It was to be directed by Berry Gordy himself, who had no experience of movie direction, and was to be based on a story by Toni Amber. Billy Dee Williams would again co-star with Diana, along with Anthony Perkins. It was to be called *Mahogany*.

In John Byrum's screenplay Tracy Chambers (Ross) rises from her ghetto upbringing in Chicago by studying fashion, her great love, in night school. After an affair with a local politician (Williams), she is discovered by a fashion photographer (Perkins). He whisks Tracy off to Rome, where his mental instability becomes manifest. He is unable to see women other than as chattels, mere wooden objects (he renames Tracy Mahogany), is impotent, and finally becomes so jealous of his protégée that he tries to kill her by crashing the car in which they are driving. He manages to kill only himself, and Mahogany is taken under the wing of a rich Italian (played by Jean-Pierre Aumont), who provides her with the money to put on a major fashion show of her own designs and become an exalted *couturière*. The Italian, of course, has an ulterior motive for all his kindness: he wants Tracy. But her hard-won fame

As (top row, far left) the sports commentators might put it – an early bath. On location in Rome, the original pose (bottom left) of Diana/Mahogany isn't good enough for photographer Perkins so he tips her into a fountain. Three coins, okay, but this is a bit much. All ends well, however, when the star is reunited with her first love, a rising politician again played by Billy Dee Williams. But not before the model sensationally turns designer (near left). Diana actually designed all her clothes for the film

can't hide the loneliness of her new life and the feeling she still has for her first and only real love, the Chicago politician. So she gives up her bright, new career and returns to the Windy City.

For her performance in this role Diana could draw on her studies of college fashion design and costume illustration and on a lifelong interest in clothes design. She persuaded Gordy to let her design the clothes Mahogany would wear and design in the movie, and the result was fifty exotic designs influenced by the costumes of the Kabuki Theatre, Japanese kite designs and the work of Erté. She worked on the gowns for nine months from March to November 1974, and shooting on the film began in Chicago towards the end of that November. The eleven-week schedule was to be split between Chicago and filming in Rome.

Diana again brought a high degree of credibility to her role for, as she pointed out, as a teenager she was much like the young Tracy Chambers, spending her spare time poring over fashion magazines and making sketches of her own designs. And she certainly had the style and glamour to capture the flowering of a young ghetto girl into a beautiful and determined woman. But the improbabilities in the plot, with Anthony Perkins playing a man so clearly and twitchily deranged almost from the start, and some less than convincing acting in the supporting roles, let the film down badly. *Mahogany* opened in the United States in late 1975 and in Britain in the spring of 1976, and although Michael Masser's score and the theme tune, 'Do You Know Where You're Going to', won an Oscar, this film never matched the critical and commercial success of her first one.

If doubts about Diana's ability to play Billie Holiday adequately had proved groundless, the similar reservations about her suitability for the role of Dorothy, the lead in *The Wiz*, would require an equally powerful performance to silence them. This black version of *The Wizard of Oz* had run on Broadway for over a year and had won seven Tonys (the Broadway equivalent of Hollywood's Oscars) including that awarded for Best Score. It was the hottest Broadway musical property for a long time and the battle to acquire the film rights was hard fought. Motown finally picked up the rights in August 1976.

On stage in New York Stephanie Mills had made the character of Dorothy her own. The Los Angeles production had seen another good performance by Ren Woods. But Mills was the favourite to land the film part. When Diana heard that Motown had the rights to *The Wiz* and that the film was already in the early stages of preparation, she played the video of the Garland screen version, which she'd bought for her children, and after watching it several times phoned Gordy. Thus began the job of persuading him that she was made for the part.

The obvious objection, which was raised immediately, was that at thirty-two going on thirty-three, she was simply too old for the part. Diana countered this argument by pointing out that the character of Dorothy in the original story by L. Frank Baum was ageless and, indeed, only sketchily drawn. She scrupulously studied an annotated *Oz*. Her persistence paid off and Gordy gave her the role. Director John Badham left the film at this time, insisting that she was too old for the part, and Sidney Lumet, who had recently directed Richard Burton in *Equus* and Peter Finch in *Network* was brought in.

For those still unfamiliar with the story of *The Wizard of Oz*, it tells the Alice in Wonderland tale of a girl and her dog who are transported, during a storm, to a strange world. The tale is built around her efforts to get back home, the characters she meets – also looking for something – and their journey together to the city of Oz, where the Wizard has the power to answer all their prayers. Dorothy and her friends – a Lion in search of courage, a Scarecrow in search of a brain, and a Tin Man in search of a heart – make the journey hindered and helped by a bad and a good witch respectively. When they finally receive their audience with the Wizard, he turns out to have lost his magic powers. Bluffing his way through their first meeting, the Wizard says he'll grant them all their wishes if they kill the bad witch (Evillene, the Wicked Witch of the North) and after a couple of stagey chases and battles they succeed.

The four return to the Wizard, stumble into his hideout and discover that the Wiz is, in fact, an imposter, a failed local politician (well, dog-catcher) who landed in Oz by mistake and was proclaimed Wiz.

Dorothy and her friends are utterly crestfallen at this and their hopes of seeing their wishes granted suddenly vanish. But our heroine explains that the way in which her three friends have behaved during their adventures together proves that the Lion has courage, the Scarecrow brains and the Tin Man a heart. Their wishes have been granted. But that doesn't help Dorothy out of her problem. Re-enter the Good Witch, Glinda, whose explanation is that if we have faith and self-belief then we'll always be at home. So after saying a tearful goodbye to her chums, Dot, who believes in herself whole-heartedly, clicks her magic shoes and is whisked home.

The original film's location was switched from a rural one to an urban setting, and the city of New York was used as backcloth for many of the scenes. The sets, including some scenes shot in the New York streets, used some twenty-five miles of yellow linoleum to depict the Yellow Brick Road which the friends had to follow to reach Oz. The Chrysler Building, Queen's Festival Theatre and the World Trade Centre were all used as set-pieces.

The supporting cast included Richard Pryor as the Wiz, Michael Jackson as Scarecrow (he and the Jacksons, except Jermaine, had by then left Motown for Epic Records) and Lena Horne as Glinda, plus Nipsey Russell (The Tin Man), Ted Ross (The Lion) and Mabel King (Evillene), the last two retaining their Broadway stage roles.

The stage *Wiz* had been scored by Charlie Smalls, and he and producer Lumet spent months persuading songwriter/record producer Quincy Jones to handle the soundtrack. After much indecision Jones took the plunge, added four new tunes of his own, and the film and music started rehearsals in July 1977. With an enormous cast of extras, including 120 dancers and 105 singers plus 300 musicians working on the charts of nine orchestrators under three conductors, this was clearly going to be a long, complicated and expensive production. And so it was.

The film over-ran its schedule and the original reported $30 million budget was said to have been exceeded by some $10 million. With promotion expenses at an estimated $4.5 million, the film had a final break-even target of $60 million. Although ticket prices had increased, the fact remained that

Munchkins, Flying Monkies, Winkies, Crows and Evillene, the Wicked Witch of the North are all about to be obliterated as Diana/Dorothy emerges triumphant from the Land of Oz . . . and this book

Diana's first, much-praised movie had reputedly grossed in the region of $10 million. Looking at the film itself it was hard to see just what all the money had been spent on. True, there were large sets and many costumes, but none of them looked outrageously expensive. Tacky, perhaps. And Diana/Dorothy's costumes were kept deliberately simple to contrast with the garish togs surrounding her. In fact, the film cost more like $24 million to make, with $13.5 million spent on North American rentals.

The film was premièred in New York and Los Angeles simultaneously towards the end of 1978 and opened in London at the beginning of the next year. It was a severe box office failure and in terms of expenditure confirmed the adage that more equalled less. The soundtrack double album, produced by Jones, was a much more enjoyable piece of work with several of Smalls' original tunes, especially 'Ease On Down the Road', which performed the function of the Garland film's 'Follow the Yellow Brick Road', Michael Jackson's singing of 'You Can't Win', and the final 'Believe in Yourself' standing out.

But it was Diana's least convincing film role by far and rather confirmed the impression that she was too old for the girlish role and had won it for her 'bankable' status as much as anything. To add to the minor calamity, during work on the set the lights had damaged the retinas of her eyes, and from time to time her vision is still impaired.

Since *The Wiz*, other movie roles have been offered or sought. She was spoken of as a possible co-star of *Cuba* with Sean Connery. She was set to play a co-lead in *Tough Customers*, a movie about the numbers racket in which she would play the queen of the racket. She was to co-star with Ryan O'Neal in a film called *Bodyguard* in which she would fall in love, Patty Hearst style, with the man hired to guard her. Her involvement in these projects came to nothing and in the case of *Cuba*, a poor film, and *Bodyguard*, an idea that sounds particularly awful, it can only be a matter of great relief.

Having resuscitated her recording career with Ashford and Simpson's *The Boss* and Chic's *Diana*, she must now be seriously considering a complementary revival in films, one which will re-establish her as a top box-office draw and, more importantly, a film actress of substance.

DISCOGRAPHY

The following list of American and British albums and singles covers the period March 1961 to January 1981. During that time Diana has been heard on records by the Supremes, Diana Ross and the Supremes, Diana Ross and the Supremes and the Temptations, Diana Ross, Diana Ross and Marvin Gaye, and several other miscellaneous titles such as sound-tracks, tributes and Motown 'Various Artists' collections. To avoid too much repetition, her contributions to Motown hits repackages, which would have appeared already in single or album track form, have not been listed.

The listings are: single or album title, American catalogue number, American release date, British catalogue number, British release date. Some singles were released only in America or Britain. In some instances B sides varied.

The list is reproduced by courtesy of Motown Records (EMI).

SINGLES

THE SUPREMES

'I Want a Guy'/'Never Again'	Tamla 54038 March 1961	—— ——
'Buttered Popcorn'/'Who's Loving You'	Tamla 54045 July 1961	—— ——
'Your Heart Belongs to Me'/'He's Seventeen'	Motown 1027 May 1962	—— ——
'Let Me Go the Right Way'/'Time Changes Things'	Motown 1034 November 1962	—— ——
'My Heart Can't Take No More'/ 'You Bring Back Memories'	Motown 1040 February 1963	—— ——
'Breathtaking Guy'/ (The Man with the) 'Rock 'n' Roll Banjo Band'	Motown 1044 June 1963	—— ——
'When the Lovelight Starts Shining through His Eyes'/ 'Standing at the Crossroads of Love'	Motown 1051 October 1963	Stateside 257 January 1964
'Run, Run, Run'/'I'm Giving You Your Freedom'	Motown 1054 February 1964	—— ——
'Where Did Our Love Go'/ 'He Means the World to Me'	Motown 1060 June 1964	Stateside 327 August 1964

Re-released in UK only in August 1974 on TMG 915. Also re-released in UK as double A side with 'Stop! In the Name of Love' in September 1976 on TMG 1044.

'Baby Love'/'Ask Any Girl'	Motown 1066 September 1964	Stateside 350 October 1964

Re-released in UK with 'Nothing but Heartaches' on B side in November 1974 on TMG 925.

'Come See About Me'/ (You're Gone but) 'Always in My Heart'	Motown 1068 October 1964	Stateside 376 January 1965
'Stop! In the Name of Love'/'I'm in Love Again'	Motown 1074 February 1965	Tamla Motown TMG 501 March 1965
'Back in My Arms Again'/ 'Whisper You Love Me Boy'	Motown 1075 April 1965	Tamla Motown TMG 516 May 1965
'Nothing but Heartaches'/'He Holds His Own'	Motown 1080 July 1965	Tamla Motown TMG 527 August 1965
'I Hear a Symphony'/ 'Who Could Ever Doubt My Love'	Motown 1083 October 1965	Tamla Motown TMG 543 December 1965
'Twinkle, Twinkle Little Me'/ 'Children's Christmas Song'	Motown 1085 November 1965	—— ——
'My World Is Empty without You'/ 'Everything Is Good About You'	Motown 1089 December 1965	Tamla Motown TMG 548 February 1966
'Love Is Like an Itching in My Heart'/'He's All I Got'	Motown 1094 April 1966	Tamla Motown TMG 560 May 1966

136

'You Can't Hurry Love'/ 'Put Yourself in My Place'	Motown 1097 July 1966	Tamla Motown TMG 575 September 1966
'You Keep Me Hangin' On'/ 'Remove This Doubt'	Motown 1101 October 1966	Tamla Motown TMG 585 November 1966
'Love Is Here and Now You're Gone'/ 'There's No Stopping Us Now'	Motown 1103 January 1967	Tamla Motown TMG 597 February 1967
'The Happening'/'All I Know about You'	Motown 1107 March 1967	Tamla Motown TMG 607 May 1967

DIANA ROSS AND THE SUPREMES

'Reflections'/'Going Down for the Third Time'	Motown 1111 July 1967	Tamla Motown TMG 616 August 1967
'In and Out of Love'/ 'I Guess I'll Always Love You'	Motown 1116 October 1967	Tamla Motown TMG 632 November 1967
'Forever Came Today'/'Time Changes Things'	Motown 1122 February 1968	Tamla Motown TMG 650 April 1968
'Some Things You Never Get Used To'/ 'You've Been So Wonderful to Me'	Motown 1126 May 1968	Tamla Motown TMG 662 June 1968
'Love Child'/'Will This Be the Day'	Motown 1135 September 1968	Tamla Motown TMG 677 November 1969
'I'm Living in Shame'/ 'I'm So Glad I Got Somebody' (like You around)	Motown 1139 January 1969	Tamla Motown TMG 695 April 1969
'The Composer'/'The Beginning of the End'	Motown 1146 March 1969	—— ——
'No Matter What Sign You Are'/ 'The Young Folks'	Motown 1148 May 1969	Tamla Motown TMG 704 July 1969
'Someday We'll Be Together'/ 'He's My Sunny Boy'	Motown 1156 October 1969	Tamla Motown TMG 721 November 1969

Re-released with 'You Keep Me Hangin' On' as double A side in August 1977 on TMG 1080.

DIANA ROSS AND THE SUPREMES AND THE TEMPTATIONS

'I'm Gonna Make You Love Me'/ 'A Place in the Sun'	Motown 1137 December 1968	Tamla Motown TMG 685 January 1969

Re-released in UK with Marvin Gaye's 'I Heard It through the Grapevine' on TMG 1045 in September 1976.

'I'll Try Something New'/ 'The Way You Do the Things You Do'	Motown 1142 February 1969	—— ——
'The Weight'/'For Better or Worse'	Motown 1153 August 1969	—— ——
'I Second That Emotion'/ 'The Way You Do the Things You Do'	—— ——	Tamla Motown TMG 709 September 1969
'Why Must We Fall in Love'/ 'Uptight (Everything's Alright)'	—— ——	Tamla Motown TMG 730 March 1970

DIANA ROSS

'Reach Out and Touch (Somebody's Hand)'/ 'Dark Side of the World'	Motown 1165 April 1970	Tamla Motown TMG 743 June 1970
'Ain't No Mountain High Enough'/ 'Can't It Wait until Tomorrow'	Motown 1169 July 1970	Tamla Motown TMG 751 August 1970
'Remember Me'/'How About You'	Motown 1176 December 1970	Tamla Motown TMG 768 March 1971
'Reach Out, I'll Be There'/ 'They Long to Be Close to You'	Motown 1184 April 1974	'Reach Out, I'll Be There'/ —— ——

Title	Motown (US)	Tamla Motown (UK)
'Surrender'/'I'm a Winner'	Motown 1188 July 1971	Tamla Motown TMG 792 October 1971
'I'm Still Waiting'/'A Simple Thing Like Cry' (UK B side: 'Reach Out, I'll Be There')	Motown 1192 October 1971	Tamla Motown TMG 781 August 1971 Re-released with 'Touch Me in the Morning' as double A side, UK only, on TMG 1041 in September 1976.
'Doobedoodn'Doobe, Doobedoodn'Doobe, Doobedoodn'Doo'/'Keep an Eye'	—— ——	Tamla Motown TMG 812 April 1972
'Good Morning Heartache'/'God Bless the Child'	Motown 1211 December 1972	Tamla Motown TMG 849 March 1973
'Touch Me in the Morning'/'I Won't Last a Day Without You' (UK B side: 'Baby It's Love')	Motown 1239 May 1973	Tamla Motown TMG 861 July 1973
'All of My Life'/'A Simple Thing Like Cry'	—— ——	Tamla Motown TMG 880 November 1973
'Last Time I Saw Him'/'Save the Children' (UK B side: 'Everything Is Everything')	Motown 1278 December 1973	Tamla Motown TMG 893 April 1974
'Sleepin''/'You'	Motown 1295 April 1974	—— ——
'Love Me'/'Save the Children'	—— ——	Tamla Motown TMG 917 September 1974
'Sorry Doesn't Always Make It Right'/'Together'	Motown 1335 February 1975	Tamla Motown TMG 941 February 1975
Theme from *Mahogany* – 'Do You Know Where You're Going To'/'No One's Gonna Be a Fool Forever'	Motown 1377 September 1975	Tamla Motown TMG 1010 October 1975
'Thought It Took a Little Time (but Today I Fell in Love)'/'After You'	Motown 1387 February 1976	Tamla Motown TMG 1032 July 1976
'Love Hangover'/'Kiss Me Now'	Motown 1392 March 1976	Tamla Motown TMG 1024 April 1976 After release in UK of this single the Tamla Motown label was stopped and all subsequent singles came out on a redesigned Motown label.
'One Love in My Lifetime'/'Smile' (UK B side: 'You're Good My Child').	Motown 1398 July 1976	Motown TMG 1056 October 1976
'Gettin' Ready for Love'/'Confide in Me' (UK B side: 'Stone Liberty')	Motown 1427 October 1977	Motown TMG 1090 October 1977
'Your Love Is So Good for Me'/'Baby It's Me'	Motown 1436 January 1978	Motown TMG 1104 April 1978
'Top of the World'/'Too Shy to Say'	—— ——	Motown TMG 1099 February 1978
'You Got It'/'Too Shy to Say'	Motown 1442 June 1978	—— ——
'Lovin', Livin' and Givin''/'You Got It'	—— ——	Motown TMG 1112 July 1978
'What You Gave Me'/'Together' (UK B side: 'Ain't No Mountain High Enough')	Motown 1456 December 1978	Motown TMG 1135 February 1979
'The Boss'/'I'm in the World'	Motown 1462 May 1979	Motown TMG 1150 June 1979
'No One Gets the Prize'/'Never Say I Don't Love You'	—— ——	Motown TMG 1160 September 1979
'It's My House'/'Sparkle'	Motown 1471 October 1979	Motown TMG 1169 November 1979
'Upside Down'/'Friend to Friend'	Motown 1494 June 1980	Motown TMG 1195 July 1980
'My Old Piano'/'Where Did We Go Wrong'	—— ——	Motown TMG 1202 September 1980
'I'm Coming Out'/'Friend to Friend' (UK B side: 'Give Up')	Motown 1491 August 1980	Motown TMG 1210 November 1980
'It's My Turn'/'Together' (UK B side: 'Sleepin'')	Motown 1496 September 1980	Motown TMG 1217 January 1981
'One More Chance'/'After You' (UK B side: 'Confide in Me')	Motown 1308 February 1981	Motown TMG 1227 March 1981

DIANA ROSS AND MARVIN GAYE

'You're a Special Part of Me'/ 'I'm Falling in Love with You'	Motown 1280 September 1973	Tamla Motown TMG 879 November 1973
'My Mistake (Was to Love You)'/'Include Me in Your Life' (UK B side: 'Just Say, Just Say')	Motown 1269 January 1974	Tamla Motown TMG 920 October 1974
'You Are Everything'/'Include Me in Your Life'	— —	Tamla Motown TMG 890 March 1974

Re-released in UK only with B side of Marvin Gaye and Tammi Terrell on Motown TMG 1047 in September 1976.

'Don't Knock My Love'/'Just Say, Just Say' (UK B side: 'I'm Falling in Love with You')	Motown 1296 June 1974	Tamla Motown TMG 953 July 1975
'Stop, Look, Listen (to Your Heart)'/'Love Twins'	— —	Tamla Motown TMG 906 June 1974

DIANA ROSS, MARVIN GAYE, STEVIE WONDER AND SMOKEY ROBINSON

'Pops We Love You'/'Pops We Love You' (instrumental)	Motown 1455 December 1978	Motown TMG 1136 February 1979

ALBUMS

THE SUPREMES

Meet the Supremes	Motown 606 March 1963	Stateside SL 10109 October 1964
Where Did Our Love Go	Motown 621 August 1964	— —
A Little Bit of Liverpool (UK title: *With Love (from Us to You)*)	Motown 623 December 1964	Tamla Motown TML 11002 March 1965
The Supremes Sing Country, Western and Pop	Motown 625 March 1965	Tamla Motown TML 11018 October 1965
We Remember Sam Cooke	Motown 629 April 1965	Tamla Motown TML 11012 July 1965
More Hits	Motown 627 July 1965	Tamla Motown TML 11020 December 1965
At the Copa (Live!)	Motown 636 November 1965	Tamla Motown STML 11026 February 1966
Merry Christmas	Motown 638 November 1965	— —
I Hear a Symphony	Motown 643 February 1966	Tamla Motown STML 11028 June 1966
Supremes a Go Go	Motown 649 August 1966	Tamla Motown STML 11039 December 1966
Sing Holland-Dozier-Holland (UK title: *Supremes Sing Motown*)	Motown 650 January 1967	Tamla Motown STML 11047 May 1967
Sing Rodgers and Hart	Motown 659 May 1967	Tamla Motown STML 11054 September 1967
Greatest Hits Vols. 1 and 2 (double LP; in UK issued as a single LP, *Greatest Hits*)	Motown 663 August 1967	Tamla Motown STML 11063 January 1968

DIANA ROSS AND THE SUPREMES

Reflections	Motown 665 March 1968	Tamla Motown STML 11073 July 1968
Sing and Perform Funny Girl	Motown 672 August 1968	Tamla Motown STML 11088 February 1969
Love Child	Motown 670 January 1969	Tamla Motown STML 11095 January 1969
Live at London's Talk of the Town	Motown 676 August 1968	Tamla Motown STML 11070 April 1968
Let the Sunshine in	Motown 689 May 1969	Tamla Motown STML 11114 November 1969
Cream of the Crop	Motown 694 November 1969	Tamla Motown STML 11137 February 1970
Greatest Hits Vol. 3 (UK title: *Greatest Hits Vol. 2*)	Motown 702 December 1969	Tamla Motown STML 11146 May 1970
Farewell (double album)	Motown 708 April 1970	Tamla Motown STML 11154/5 August 1970
Baby Love	—— ——	Sounds Superb SPR 90001 September 1973
Anthology (triple album in US; double in UK)	Motown 794 July 1974	Tamla Motown TMSP 6001 October 1975
Motown Special – Diana Ross and the Supremes	—— ——	Motown STMX 6001 March 1977
20 Golden Greats	—— ——	Motown EMTV5 August 1977

DIANA ROSS AND THE SUPREMES AND THE TEMPTATIONS

Diana Ross and the Supremes Join the Temptations	Motown 679 November 1968	Tamla Motown STML 11096 January 1969
TCB (TV special soundtrack)	Motown 682 December 1968	Tamla Motown STML 11110 July 1969
	Re-released in US only on Natural Resources NR4020T1 in August 1979	
Together	Motown 692 September 1969	Tamla Motown STML 11122 February 1970
On Broadway	Motown 699 November 1969	—— ——
Motown Special – Diana Ross and the Supremes and the Temptations	—— ——	Motown STMX 6003 March 1977

DIANA ROSS

Diana Ross	Motown 711 May 1970	Tamla Motown STML 11159 October 1970
Everything Is Everything	Motown 724 October 1970	Tamla Motown STML 11178 April 1971
Diana! (TV special soundtrack)	Motown 719 March 1971	Tamla Motown STMA 8001 November 1971
Surrender	Motown 723 July 1971	—— ——
I'm Still Waiting	—— ——	Tamla Motown STML 11193 October 1971
Greatest Hits	—— ——	Tamla Motown STMA 8006 October 1972
Lady Sings the Blues (movie soundtrack, double album)	Motown 758 December 1972	Tamla Motown TMSP 1131 March 1973

Touch Me in the Morning	Motown 772 June 1973	Tamla Motown STML 11239 August 1973
Last Time I Saw Him	Motown 812 December 1973	Tamla Motown STML 11255 February 1974
Live! At Caesar's Palace (UK title: *Live!*)	Motown 801 May 1974	Tamla Motown STML 11248 July 1974
Original Soundtrack of Mahogany	Motown 858 October 1975	Tamla Motown STML 12004 November 1975
Diana Ross	Motown 861 February 1976	Tamla Motown STML 12022 March 1976
Greatest Hits	Motown 869 July 1976	—— ——
Greatest Hits/2	—— ——	Tamla Motown STML 12036 July 1976
An Evening with . . . (double album)	Motown 877 January 1977	Motown TMSP 6005 February 1977
	In UK all albums hereafter on redesigned Motown label.	
Baby It's Me	Motown 890 September 1977	Motown STMA 8031 October 1977
Ross	Motown 907 September 1978	Motown STML 12093 October 1978
The Boss	Motown 923 May 1979	Motown STML 12118 June 1979
20 Golden Greats	—— ——	Motown EMTV 21 November 1979
Diana	Motown 936 May 1980	Motown STMA 8033 June 1980
To Love Again	Motown 951 February 1981	Motown STML 12152 March 1981

DIANA ROSS AND MARVIN GAYE

Diana and Marvin	Motown 803 October 1973	Tamla Motown STMA 8015 September 1973

MISCELLANEOUS

Diana Ross also appears on many Motown repackages and on the *Original Motion Picture Soundtrack: The Wiz* (MCA double album MCSP 287) from 1978 and *Music from the Original Motion Picture Soundtrack: It's My Turn* (Motown US 947) from 1980 and *Original Motion Picture Sooundtrack of* Thank God It's Friday (Casablanca TGIF 100).

INDEX

PHOTO ACKNOWLEDGEMENTS

The author and publishers are grateful to the following for providing and/or granting permission to reproduce the illustrations on the pages listed:

Associated Newspapers, 38 *bottom right*, 53 *left*; Keith Bernstein, 85 *top left*; *Black Music*, 1, 25, 26 *right*, 29, 51, 66, 86-7 (Paramount Pictures), 87 *top*, *centre and bottom* (Paramount Pictures), 88 *left*, 100-1, 113, 122, 122-3, 124-5, 130-1, 132; *Daily Mirror,* 41 *right*; E.M.I., 7 *top right,* 8-9, 34-5, 38 *top right,* 40, 54-5, 55; H. Goodwin, 7 *top left*; Gijsbert Hanekroot, 80; Keystone, 14-15, 58-9, 94-5 (photo by Peter L. Gould), 114 *bottom left* (photo by Sonia Moskowitz); London Features International Ltd, 84-5 *top*, 96 (photo by Paul Canty), 97 (photo by Chris Walter), 114 *top centre* (photo by Richard Creamer); *Melody Maker*, 26 *left*, 28, 34, 60, 76, 116 *top and bottom*, 118-19; Gary Merrin, 67 *right*; Motown, 10 (E.M.I.), 53 *right*, 72-3, 77 (E.M.I.), 104 *bottom* (E.M.I., photo by Douglas Kirkland), 106-7 (E.M.I.), 108, 110 (E.M.I.), 112 (E.M.I.); Terry O'Neill, 104 *top*; Paramount Pictures, 120, 121; Jan Persson, 42-3, 56; Pictorial Press Ltd, 93; Barry Plummer, 45; Popperfoto, 13, 18 *bottom*, 22-3, 47 (Associated Newspapers), 63, 75, 90-1, 98, 99 *left and right*, 111, 114 *top left*, 130 *top right and centre*; David Redfern, 82-3, 84-5 *bottom* (photo by Richard E. Aaron), 103; Rex Features, 2-3 (photo by Sergio Strizzi, Distr. Fòrum), 12-13 (photo by David Magnus), 16, 19, 30-1, 32 (photo by Feri Lukas), 33 (photo by Feri Lukas), 44, 50 *bottom*, 57 (photo by Brian Moody), 78-9 (photo by Patrick Frilet, S.I.P.A. Press), 79 (photo by Patrick Frilet, S.I.P.A. Press), 81 *top left*, 102, 105 (photo by Jeanmeau, S.I.P.A. Press), 114-15 *top* (photo by Villard-Barthelmy, S.I.P.A. Press), 114-15 *bottom* (photo by Barthelmy, S.I.P.A. Press), 117 (photo by Patrick Frilet, S.I.P.A. Press), 126-7 (photo by Sergio Strizzi, Distr. Fòrum), 128-9 (photo by Sergio Strizzi, Distr. Fòrum), 129 (photo by Sergio Strizzi, Distr. Fòrum), 134-5; Marc Sharratt, Photography 33, 20-1, 35; S.K.R. Photos International Ltd, 39, 81 *bottom*, Sport and General, 24; Peter Stuart, 27; Syndication International Ltd, 6, 7 *top centre and bottom right*, 62-3, 64, 65, 67 *left*, 68, 69, 70-1, 81 *top right*, 83 *top and bottom*, 85 *top right*, 88 *right*, 89, 92, 108-9, 130 *top right*, 131; Thomson Newspapers Ltd, 18 *top*; United Press International (U.K.) Ltd, 41 *left*, 46, 48-9; Barrie Wentzell, 36-7; Valerie Wilmer, 38 *top left*, Bernard Yeszin, 50 *top*.